The Negro in the Continental Congress, 1774-1789

Extracts from the 34 volumes of the Journals of the Continental Congress, 1774-1789. Edited from the original records in the Library of Congress by Worthington Chauncey Ford, Gaillard Hunt, John C. Fitzpatrick and Roscoe R. Hill, Division of Manuscripts, Washington, Government Printing Office, 1904-1937.

T H E

Association, &c.

WE, his Majeſty's moſt loyal ſubjects, the Delegates of the ſeveral Colonies of New-Hampſhire, Maſſachuſett's Bay, Rhode-Iſland, Connecticut, New-York, New-Jerſey, Pennſylvania, the Three Lower Counties of Newcaſtle, Kent, and Suſſex, on Delaware, Maryland, Virginia, North-Carolina, and South-Carolina, deputed to repreſent them in a continental Congreſs, held in the city of Philadelphia, on the fifth day of September, 1774, avowing our allegiance to his Majeſty, our affection and regard for our fellow-ſubjects in Great-Britain and elſewhere, affected with the deepeſt anxiety, and moſt alarming apprehenſions at thoſe grievances and diſtreſſes, with which his Majeſty's American ſubjects are oppreſſed, and having taken under our moſt ſerious deliberation, the ſtate of the whole continent, find, that the preſent unhappy ſituation of our affairs, is occaſioned by a ruinous ſyſtem of colony adminiſtration adopted by the Britiſh Mi-

A niſtry

The Association of 1774
Frontispiece

THE NEGRO IN THE CONGRESSIONAL RECORD
Volume I:

The Negro in the Continental Congress

Compiled and annotated by
Peter M. Bergman and Jean McCarroll

BERGMAN PUBLISHERS
New York

Published, 1969, by
BERGMAN PUBLISHERS
224 West Twentieth Street
New York, N. Y. 10011

Standard Book Number: 87503-019-10
Library of Congress Catalog Card Number: 69-17560

Printed in the United States of America

Introduction

It has been the great interest in the history of the Negro in America which has recently created the demand for source material on this field. However, the facts seem to support Albert Bushnell Hart's observation on the plight of the modern historian—namely, as Hart stated routinely in his seminars at Harvard many years ago, that it is no longer possible for the historian to work directly from original sources; that on any period and subject, the materials which accumulate in a year are more than can be assimilated by one mind in three years; and that the historian must use the results of others' work. Today, about 75 years later, the student of history is even less able to find the original (now called "obscure") sources. Additionally, the tendency to avoid footnotes, even in serious historical works, sometimes merely for the sake of "appearance," has become increasingly widespread, rendering primary source material even less accessible. In fields which have been dealt with exhaustively, the student of history may find secondary works a sufficient source of information, but in spite of the new interest in the history of the Negro in America, literature on this subject is still meagre.

The intention of the present compilation is, therefore, to provide the student of American history with a primary source work on the Negro in this country. Of a total of 34 volumes of the "Journals of the Continental Congress" (comprising 14,514 pages), 153 pages are here reproduced in which dealings of the Continental Congress with the Negro problem were recorded. The entire page has in each case been reprinted in order to leave the extracts as much as possible in their original context.

Considering the fact that the debates in the Continental Congress took place over a period of 15 years, with a sum total of over 14,000 pages of record, it is in itself symptomatic that mention of the Negro occurs so rarely. Although at that time there was as yet no official "gag rule," the threat expressed by Thomas *Lynch*, the delegate from South Carolina, was explicit: "If it is *debate*d whether their (the Southern slaveholders') slaves are their property, there is an end of the confederation" (page 16 of this book).

PMB

*

The present volume is the first of a series which will comprise in its final form approximately 23 volumes on the subject of the Negro in America as it appears in the Congressional Record.

TABLE OF CONTENTS

Table of Contents

Table of Contents

any East-India tea from any part of the world; nor any molasses, syrups, paneles,[1] coffee, or pimento, from the British plantations or from Dominica; nor wines from Madeira, or the Western Islands; nor foreign indigo.

"Articles of Association" read and signed October 20, 1774

2. We will neither import nor purchase, any slave imported after the first day of December next;[2] after which time, we will wholly discontinue the slave trade, and will neither be concerned in it ourselves, nor will we hire our vessels, nor sell our commodities or manufactures to those who are concerned in it.

3. As a non-consumption agreement, strictly adhered to, will be an effectual security for the observation of the non-importation, we, as above, solemnly agree and associate, that, from this day, we will not purchase or use any tea, imported on account of the East-India company, or any on which a duty hath been or shall be paid; and from and after the first day of March next, we will not purchase or use any East-India tea whatever; nor will we, nor shall any person for or under us, purchase or use any of those goods, wares, or merchandise, we have agreed not to import, which we shall know, or have cause to suspect, were imported after the first day of December, except such as come under the rules and directions of the tenth article hereafter mentioned.

4. The earnest desire we have, not to injure our fellow-subjects in Great-Britain, Ireland, or the West-Indies, induces us to suspend a non-exportation, until the tenth day of September, 1775; at which time, if the said acts and parts of acts of the British parliament herein after mentioned are not repealed, we will not, directly or indirectly, export any merchandise or commodity whatsoever to Great-Britain, Ireland, or the West-Indies, except rice to Europe.[3]

5. Such as are merchants, and use the British and Irish trade, will give orders, as soon as possible, to their factors, agents and correspondents, in Great-Britain and Ireland, not to ship any goods to them, on any pretence whatsoever, as they cannot be received in America; and if any merchant, residing in Great-Britain or Ireland, shall directly or indirectly ship any goods, wares or merchandise, for America, in order to break the said non-importation agreement, or in any manner contravene the same, on such unworthy conduct being well attested, it ought to be made public; and, on the same being so

[1] Brown unpurified sugar.

[2] In the pamphlet edition this sentence reads: "That we will neither import, nor purchase any slave imported, after the first day of December next."

[3] See *Journals of Congress*, 1 August, 1775, *post*.

ensuing Continental Congress, as the only Means of obtaining Relief, and to put you in the Situation you wish, which this Committee apprehend to be entirely out of their Power to do; as it is their Opinion, that the Parish of St. John, being a Part of the Colony of Georgia (which, by not acceding to, has violated the Continental Association) falls under the 14th Article of the said Association, no Part of which any Committee can presume to do away, &c. &c."

Upon the Receipt of this Answer, it was seriously considered in what Manner to conduct in the present Situation; and proposed, whether we should immediately break off all Connexion and Commerce with Savannah, and all other Inhabitants of this province, who have not fully acceded to the Continental Association.

It was considered, that as we were denied Commerce with any other Colony, and but one Merchant among us considerable for dry Goods, had signed our Association, and he insufficient for a present Supply, and we utterly unable at Present to procure Materials or Manufactures for Cloathing among ourselves, we must, by such a Resolution, become extreamly miserable; it was therefore concluded, that till we could obtain Trade and Commerce with some other Colony, it is absolutely necessary to continue it in some Respects with our own, and determined that it be carryed on under the following Regulations:

Signed address from inhabitants of St. John's Parish, Georgia, dated April 13, 1775 read May 13, 1775

I[st] That None of us shall directly or indirectly purchase any Slave imported at Savannah, (large Numbers of which we understand are there expected,) till the Sense of the Congress shall be made known to us.

II[ly] That we will not trade at all with any Merchant at Savannah, or elsewhere, that will not join in our Associating Agreement, otherwise than under the Inspection of a Committee, for that Purpose appointed, and for such Things only as they shall judge necessary, and when they shall think there are necessary Reasons for so doing.

A Committee was then nominated, and appointed to sit Weekly on Thursdays, for the Purposes aforesaid.

It was then resolved, that a Delegate be sent from this Parish to the Congress, to be held at Philadelphia, in May next, and that Tuesday, the 21st of March, be appointed for chusing one.

On the said 21st of March, at a full Meeting, Lyman Hall Esq[r] was unanimously chosen, to represent and act for the Inhabitants of this Parish, as a Delegate at the General Congress, to be had in Philadelphia, in May next, who are determined faithfully to adhere to, and

Serjeant, 8⅓.
Corporals, 7½.
Bombardiers, 7.
Matrosses, 6⅚.

That the appointment of provost Marshal, waggon master, and master carpenter, be left to the commander in chief of the army, who is to fix their pay, having regard to the pay such receive in the ministerial army, and the proportion that the pay of the Officers in said army bears to the pay of our Officers.

William Tudor, Esq[r] was elected Judge Advocate of the army.

Resolved, That Michael Hillegas, and George Clymer, Esqrs. be, and they are hereby appointed, joint treasurers of the United Colonies: that the Treasurers reside in Philadelphia, and that they shall give bond, with surety, for the faithful performance of their office, in the sum of 100,000 Dollars, to John Hancock, Henry Middleton, John Dickinson, John Alsop, Thomas Lynch, Richard Henry Lee, and James Wilson, Esqrs. and the survivor of them, in trust for the United Colonies.

That the provincial Assemblies or conventions do each chuse a treasurer for their respective colonies, and take sufficient security for the faithful performance of the trust.

That each colony provide ways and means to sink its proportion of the bills ordered to be emitted by this Congress, in such manner as may be most effectual and best adapted to the condition, circumstances, and usual mode of levying taxes in such colony.

Resolution
July 29, 1775

That the proportion or quota of each colony be determined according to the number of Inhabitants, of all ages, including negroes and mulattoes in each colony; But, as

The Committee appointed to prepare an answer to General Washington's letters, reported the same, which was read and agreed to.

Ordered, That the same ||being transcribed|| be signed by the president and forwarded immediately.

The Committee appointed to examine the journal of the Congress during the last sessions, ||in order for the press,|| reported a copy, which was ordered to be read.

||*Ordered*, That the remainder be read to Morrow.||

||Adjourned to nine o'clock to Morrow.||[1]

WEDNESDAY, SEPTEMBER 27, 1775

The committee of Acco^{ts} ||Claims|| applied to the Congress for advice how to charge sundry accounts,

The same being taken into consideration,

Resolved, That the expence of kettles, canteens, and spoons, supplied to the soldiers, be charged to the Continent.

Application being made in behalf of Connecticut for a sum of money on account of sundry advances for the use of the Continent,

Resolved, That the sum of one hundred and sixty thousand dollars be paid to Connecticut, on account for supplies issued by that colony for the service of the United Colonies, to be accounted for on the exhibiting their accounts.

The Committee of Accounts laid before the Congress three accounts.

One for a balance due to Robert Erwin, waggon master, amounting to eight hundred and eighty-seven dollars and one fifteenth of a dollar.

Debate not noted in Journal, September 26, 1775

[1] "On the twenty-sixth Edward Rutledge, of South Carolina, moved the discharge of all the negroes in the army, and he was strongly supported by many of the southern delegates; but the opposition was so determined that 'he lost his point.'" Bancroft, *History of the United States*, IV, 261.

The members chosen, Mr. [Stephen] Hopkins, Mr. [Samuel] Huntington, Mr. [Robert Treat] Paine, Mr. [Lewis] Morris, and Mr. [William] Floyd.

Resolved, That the committee appointed to fit out armed vessels, be empowered to purchase and fit out a small vessel as a tender for the fleet fitted out.

The committee appointed, to devise ways and means for procuring powder from Providence, brought in a report, with an account of a cargo provided for that purpose by Messrs. Willing and Morris, amounting to £1,212.9.0 Pensylvania currency = 3,233 2/10 Dollars; Whereupon,

Resolved, That the said committee be authorized to give such orders to the captain of the vessel, fitted out for the service as they may think proper.

That an order be drawn on the treasurers, in favour of Messrs. Willing and Morris, for the sum of 3,233 2/10 dollars in full for the cargo shipped on board the sloop *Lady Catherine* for the use of the Continent.

The committee on General Washington's letters, brought in their report, which being taken into consideration, the Congress, thereupon, came to the following resolutions:

Resolved, That the pay master general of the army at Cambridge, be empowered to draw his bills upon the president of the Congress, or, in their recess, upon the committee of Congress for that purpose appointed, for any sums of money which may be deposited in his hands, not exceeding, in any one month, the monthly expences of the army; and that such bills, countersigned by the General or Commander in chief of the said army, be accepted and paid.

That the free negroes who have served faithfully in the army at Cambridge, may be re-inlisted therein, but no others.

Resolution
January 16, 1776

That, if General Washington think proper, Colonel

lars,|| be advanced to Mr. Cole, to be by him delivered to the commanding officer in Canada, for the Service of the Continent, and that he be directed to proceed immediately.

The Committee of Claims reported, that there is due,

To Dr. Jonathan Potts, for attendance on the second and fourth Pensylvania batallions, the sum of £25.6.9 = 67.6 dollars.

To Colonel Nathaniel Heard, for expences in the expedition against the tories on Long Island, the sum of £864.12.10 New York currency = 2,161.6 dollars.

Resolved, That the above be paid.

The Congress resumed the consideration of the declaration, which was agreed to as follows:

Declaration and resolution, March 23, 1776. This was printed in the Pennsylvania Gazette, March 27, 1776

Whereas the petitions of the United Colonies to the King, for the redress of great and manifest grievances, have not only been rejected, but treated with scorn and contempt, and the opposition to designs evidently formed to reduce them to a state of servile subjection, and their necessary defence against hostile forces actually employed to subdue them, declared rebellion; And whereas an unjust war hath been commenced against them, which the commanders of the British fleets and armies have prosecuted, and still continue to prosecute, with their utmost vigour, and in a cruel manner; wasting, spoiling, and destroying the country, burning houses and defenceless towns, and exposing the helpless inhabitants to every misery, from the inclemency of the winter; and not only urging savages to invade the country, but instigating negroes to murder their masters; And whereas the parliament of Great Britain hath lately passed an Act, affirming these colonies to be in open rebellion, forbidding all trade and commerce with the inhabitants thereof, until they shall accept pardons, and submit to despotic rule, declaring their property, wherever found upon the water,

number of shaken or knocked down molasses casks, than the same vessel is capable of carrying when they shall be filled with Molasses.

Resolved, That any goods, wares, and merchandise, except such as are of the growth, production, or manufacture of, or brought from any country under the dominion of the King of Great Britain, and except East India Tea, may be imported from any other parts of the world to the thirteen United Colonies, by the inhabitants thereof, and by the people of all such countries as are not subject to the said King; liable, however, to all such duties and impositions as now are, or may hereafter be laid by any of the said colonies.

Resolved, That nothing herein contained shall be understood to prevent such future commercial regulations as shall be thought just and necessary by these United Colonies, or their respective legislatures.

Resolved, That no slaves be imported into any of the thirteen United Colonies.

Resolution, April 6, 1776

Resolved, That it be recommended to the assemblies and conventions in the several colonies, to appoint proper officers, at convenient places in their respective colonies, to take bonds, in adequate penalties, for observing the regulations made by the Congress, or assemblies, or conventions, concerning trade, and for securing the observation of such parts of the association as are not inconsistent therewith; and that the obligor shall, within eighteen months after the departure of the vessel, produce to such officers a certificate, under the hands and seals of three or more reputable merchants, residing at the port or place where the cargo shall be delivered, that the same was there unladed, and take manifests upon oath, of the cargoes exported and imported, and keep fair accounts and entries thereof, give bills of health when desired, grant

Volume V
page 498

Journals of Congress

Two drafts of the Declaration of Independence, reported June 28, 1776. The black lines and brackets indicate words struck out by Congress

He has waged cruel War against human Nature itself, violating its most sacred Rights of Life and Liberty in the Persons of a distant People who never offended him, captivating and carrying them into Slavery in another Hemisphere, or to incur miserable Death, in their Transportation thither. This piratical Warfare, the opprobrium of infidel Powers, is the Warfare of the Christian King of Great Britain.

He has prostituted his Negative for Suppressing every legislative Attempt to prohibit or to restrain an execrable Commerce, determined to keep open a Markett where Men should be bought and sold. and that this assemblage of Horrors might want no Fact of distinguished Die

He is now exciting those very People to rise in Arms among us, and to purchase their Liberty of which he has deprived them, by murdering the People upon whom he also obtruded them: thus paying off, former Crimes committed against the Liberties of one People, with Crimes which he urges them to commit against the Lives of another.

on the high seas to bear arms against their country, ~~& to destroy & be destroyed by the brethren whom they love,~~ to become the executioners of their friends & brethren, or to fall themselves by their hands:

he has waged cruel war against human nature itself, violating it's most sacred rights of life & liberty in the persons of a distant people, who never offended him, captivating & carrying them into slavery in another hemisphere, or to incur miserable death in their transportation thither. this piratical warfare, the opprobrium of *infidel* powers, is the warfare of the CHRISTIAN king of Great Britain determined to keep open a market where MEN should be bought & sold, ~~and~~ he has prostituted his negative for suppressing every legislative attempt to prohibit or to restrain this execrable commerce ~~determining to keep open a market where MEN should be bought and sold~~: and that this assemblage of horrors might want no fact of distinguished dye, he is now exciting those very people to rise in arms among us, and to purchase that liberty of which *he* has deprived them, by murdering the people upon whom *he* also obtruded them: thus paying off former crimes committed against the *liberties* of one people, with crimes which he urges them to commit against the *lives* of another.]

For depriving us, in many cases, of the benefits of Trial by Jury:

For transporting us beyond Seas to be tried for pretended offences:

For abolishing the free System of English Laws in a neighbouring province, establishing therein an Arbitrary government, and enlarging its Boundaries, so as to render it at once an example and fit instrument for introducing the same absolute rule into these Colonies:

For taking away our Charters, abolishing our most valuable Laws, and altering fundamentally the Forms of our Governments:

For suspending our own Legislatures, and declaring themselves invested with Power to legislate for us in all cases whatsoever.

He has abdicated Government here, by declaring us out of his protection, and waging War against us.

He has plundered our seas, ravaged our Coasts, burnt our towns, and destroyed the Lives of our People.

He is at this time transporting large Armies of foreign Mercenaries to compleat the works of death, desolation and tyranny, already begun with circumstances of Cruelty and perfidy scarcely paralleled in the most barbarous ages, and totally unworthy the Head of a civilized nation.

He has constrained our fellow Citizens, taken Captive on the high Seas, to bear Arms against their Country, to become the executioners of their friends and Brethren, or to fall themselves by their Hands.

He has excited domestic insurrections amongst us, and has endeavoured to bring on the inhabitants of our frontiers, the merciless Indian Savages, whose known rule of warfare, is an undistinguished destruction of all ages, sexes and conditions.

Final form of Declaration of Independence, with indirect reference to slave question discussed more fully in earlier drafts, signed July 4, 1776

In every stage of these Oppressions, We have Petitioned for Redress, in the most humble terms: Our

hereafter entered into by the United States assembled, with the King or Kingdom of Great Britain, or any foreign Prince or State.

Art. IX. No standing Army or Body of Forces shall be kept up by any Colony or Colonies in Times of Peace, except such a Number only as may be requisite to garrison the Forts necessary for the Defence of such Colony or Colonies: But every Colony shall always keep up a well regulated and disciplined Militia, sufficiently armed and accoutred; and shall provide and constantly have ready for Use in public Stores, a due Number of Field Pieces and Tents, and a proper Quantity of Ammunition, and ~~other~~ Camp Equipage.[1]

Art. X. When Troops are raised in any of the Colonies for the common Defence, the Commission Officers proper for the Troops raised in each Colony, except the General Officers, shall be appointed by the Legislature of each Colony respectively, or in such manner as shall by them be directed.

Committee draft of Articles of Confederation, July 12, 1776

Art. XI. All Charges of Wars and all other Expences that shall be incurred for the common Defence, or general Welfare, and allowed by the United States ~~in General Congress~~ assembled, shall be defrayed out of a common Treasury, which shall be supplied by the several Colonies in Proportion to the Number of Inhabitants of every Age, Sex and Quality, except Indians not paying Taxes, in each Colony, a true Account of which, distinguishing the white[2] Inhabitants ~~who are not slaves,~~ shall be triennially taken and transmitted to ~~Congress~~ the Assembly of the United States. The Taxes for paying that Proportion shall be laid and levied by the Authority and Direction of the Legislatures of the several Colonies, within the Time agreed upon by United States assembled.[3]

Art. XII. Every Colony shall abide by the Determinations of the United States ~~in General Congress~~ assembled, concerning the Services performed and Losses or Expences incurred by every Colony for the common Defence or general Welfare, and no Colony or Colonies shall in any Case whatever endeavor by Force to procure Redress of any Injury or Injustice supposed to be done by the United States to such Colony or Colonies in not granting such Satisfactions, Indemnifica-

[1] "Q. Should not this Article specify the Particulars, as to Age, Arms, Field pieces, &c." *J. D.*

[2] This word was inserted on striking out "who are not slaves."

[3] "Q. If no Notice should be taken of the Bills already emitted, and if there should not be a Contract to contribute in due Proportion towards sinking them?" *J. D.*

tions, Compensations, Retributions, Exemptions, or Benefits of any Kind, as such Colony or Colonies may think just or reasonable.

Art. XIII. No Colony or Colonies shall engage in any War without the previous Consent of the United States assembled, unless such Colony or Colonies be actually invaded by Enemies, or shall have received certain Advice of a Resolution being formed by some Nations of Indians to invade such Colony or Colonies, and the Danger is so imminent, as not to admit of a Delay, till the other Colonies can be consulted: Nor shall any Colony or Colonies grant Commissions to any Ships or Vessels of War, nor Letters of Marque or Reprisal, except it be after a Declaration of War by the United States assembled, and then only against the Kingdom or State and the Subjects thereof, against which War has been so declared, and under such Regulations as shall be established by the United States assembled.[1]

Art. XIV. A perpetual Alliance, offensive and defensive, is to be entered into by the United States assembled as soon as may be, with the Six Nations, and all other neighbouring Nations of Indians; their Limits to be ascertained, their Lands to be secured to them, and not encroached on;[2] no Purchases of Lands, hereafter to be made of the Indians by Colonies or private Persons before the Limits of the Colonies are ascertained, to be valid: All Purchases of Lands not included within those Limits, where ascertained, to be made by Contracts between the United States assembled, or by Persons for that Purpose authorized by them, and the great Councils of the Indians, for the general Benefit of all the United Colonies.[3]

Art. XV. When the Boundaries of any Colony shall be ascertained by Agreement, or in the Manner herein after directed, all the other Colonies shall guarantee to such Colony the full and peaceable Possession of, and the free and entire Jurisdiction in and over the Territory included within such Boundaries.[4]

Art. XVI. For the more convenient Management of the general Interests of the United States, Delegates should be annually appointed in such Manner as the Legislature of each Colony shall direct, ~~or such~~

[1] "Q. How far the Expence of any War is to be defrayed by the Union?" *J. D.*

[2] "Q. How far a Colony may interfere in Indian Affairs?" *J. D.*

To this point this paragraph was omitted in the printed version.

[3] "This Article is submitted to Congress." *J. D.*

[4] "This Article is submitted to Congress.

"Q. Should there not be an Article to prevent those who are hereafter brought into these Colonies, from being held in Slavery within the Colonies?" *J. D.*

John Dickinson's note on the draft of the Articles of Confederation, read July 12, 1776

those Colonies, which by Charter or Proclamation, or under any Pretence, are said to extend to the South Sea, and ascertaining those Bounds of any other Colony that appear to be indeterminate—Assigning Territories for new Colonies, either in Lands to be thus separated from Colonies and heretofore purchased or obtained by the Crown of Great-Britain from the Indians, or hereafter to be purchased or obtained from them—Disposing of all such Lands for the general Benefit of all the United Colonies—Ascertaining Boundaries to such new Colonies, within which Forms of Government are to be established on the Principles of Liberty[1]—Establishing and regulating Post-Offices throughout all the United Colonies, on the Lines of Communication from one Colony to another—Appointing General Officers of the Land Forces in the Service of the United States—Commissioning such other Officers of the said Forces as shall be appointed by Virtue of the tenth Article—Appointing all the Officers of the Naval Forces in the Service of the United States—Making Rules for the Government and Regulation of the said Land and Naval Forces, and directing the ~~Marches, Cruises and~~ operations ~~of such land and naval Forces~~—Appointing a Council of State, and such Committees and civil Officers as may be necessary for managing the general Affairs of the United States, under their Direction while assembled, and in their Recess, of the Council of State—Appointing one of their number to preside, and a suitable Person for Secretary—And adjourning to any Time within the Year.

Article XVIII of committee draft of the Articles of Confederation, read July 12, 1776

The United States assembled shall have Authority for the Defence and Welfare of the United Colonies and every of them, to agree upon and fix the necessary Sums and Expences—To emit Bills, or to borrow Money on the Credit of the United Colonies—To raise Naval Forces—To agree upon the Number of Land Forces to be raised, and to make Requisitions from the Legislature of each Colony, or the Persons therein authorized by the Legislature to execute such Requisitions, for the Quota of each Colony, which is to be in Proportion to the Number of white Inhabitants in that Colony ~~who are not slaves~~, which Requisitions shall be binding, and thereupon the Legislature of each Colony or the Persons authorized as aforesaid, shall appoint the Regimental Officers, ~~and~~ raise the Men, and arm and equip them in a soldier-like Manner; and the Officers and Men so armed and equipped, shall march to the Place appointed, and within the Time agreed on by the United States assembled.

[1] "These clauses [from Limiting the Bounds, &c.] are submitted to Congress." *J. D.*

Two drafts of the Articles of Confederation, considered August 20, 1776. The left column has the first printed version. The right column shows changes made for the second printed form

sembled, shall be defrayed out of a common Treasury, which shall be supplied by the several Colonies in Proportion to the Number of Inhabitants of every Age, Sex and Quality except Indians not paying Taxes, in each Colony, a true Account of which, distinguishing the white Inhabitants shall be triennially taken and transmitted to the Assembly of the United States. The Taxes for paying that Proportion shall be laid and levied by the Authority and Direction of the Legislatures of the several Colonies, within the Time agreed upon by the United States assembled.[1]

ART. XII. Every Colony shall abide by the Determinations of the United States assembled, concerning the Services performed and Losses or Expences incurred by every Colony for the common Defence or general Welfare, and no Colony or Colonies shall in any Case whatever endeavor by Force to procure Redress of any Injury or Injustice supposed to be done by the United States to such Colony or Colonies in not granting such Satisfactions, Indemnifications, Compensations, Retributions, Exemptions, or Benefits of any Kind, as such Colony or Colonies may think just or reasonable.

a common treasury, which shall be supplied by the several States in proportion to the number of inhabitants of every age, sex and quality except Indians not paying taxes, in each State, a true account of which, distinguishing the white inhabitants shall be triennially taken and transmitted to the Assembly of the United States. The taxes for paying that proportion shall be laid and levied by the authority and direction of the legislatures of the several States, within the time agreed upon by the United States Assembled.

ART. X. Every State shall abide by the determinations of the United States in Congress Assembled, on all questions which by this Confederation are submitted to them.

[1] On the Dickinson manuscript Thomson wrote first "Postponed" and then "agreed" against this article.

That the allowance to officers of $1^1/_3$ dollars ~~bounty~~ for enlisting soldiers be not extended or given on the reinlistment of the soldiers in camp.[1]

That no officer, holding two appointments in the continental army, be paid for more than one, after notice was given to the commanders of the respective armies, of the resolution of Congress against officers holding double commissions.

Resolved, That a committee of three be appointed to devise ways and means for supplying the treasury with a farther sum of money:

The members chosen, Mr. R[ichard] H[enry] Lee, Mr. [James] Wilson, and Mr. [Lyman] Hall.

Resolution, October 14, 1776

Resolved, That a committee of three be appointed, to consider what is to be done with negroes taken by vessels of war, in the service of the United States:

The members chosen, Mr. [James] Wilson, Mr. R[ichard] H[enry] Lee, and Mr. [Samuel] Huntington.

Resolved, That 600 dollars be advanced to Mr. R. Erwin, waggon master; he to be accountable.

Resolved, That the Board of War be directed to give orders to the Virginia troops, on their march to New York, to halt at Trenton, till farther orders.

Resolved, That the colonels of the New Jersey militia, make out regular pay rolls of such of the troops as have been under their command, when called into the continental service, and have not been paid by the convention of the said state:

That one penny a mile be allowed, in lieu of rations, to such men as have paid their expences while on their march to and from the camp, from and to their respective homes.

That such rolls be attested by the oaths of the commanding officer and captains of the respective regiments,

[1] "Repealed Nov." is written in the margin.

to the Indians. "We are stronger, we are better, we treat you better than another Colony." No power ought to treat with the Indians, but the United States. Indians know the striking benefits of confederation; they have an example of it in the union of the Six Nations. The idea of the union of the Colonies struck them forcibly last year. None should trade with Indians without a license from Congress. A perpetual war would be unavoidable, if everybody was allowed to trade with them.

Stone. This expedient is worse than either of the alternatives. What is the meaning of this superintendency? Colonies will claim the right first. Congress can't interpose until the evil has happened. Disputes will arise when Congress shall interpose.

JULY 30, 1776

Article 17. "In determining questions, each Colony shall have one vote."

Dr. Franklin.[1] Let the smaller Colonies give equal money and men, and then have an equal vote. But if they have an equal vote without bearing equal burthens, a confederation upon such iniquitous principles will never last long.

Dr. Witherspoon.[2] We all agree that there must and shall be a confederation, for this war. It will diminish the glory of our object, and depreciate our hope; it will damp the ardor of the people. The greatest danger we have, is of disunion among ourselves. Is it not plausible that the small States will be oppressed by the great ones? The Spartans and Helotes. The Romans and their dependents. Every Colony is a distinct person. States of Holland.

Clark. We must apply for pardons if we don't confederate.

Wilson. We should settle upon some plan of representation.

John Adams' Notes of Debates, July 30 and August 1, 1776

Chase.[3] Moves that the word "white," should be inserted in the eleventh Article. The negroes are wealth. Numbers are not a certain rule of wealth. It is the best rule we can lay down. Negroes a species of property, personal estate. If negroes are taken into the computation of numbers to ascertain wealth, they ought to be, in settling the representation. The Massachusetts fisheries, and navigation, ought to be taken into consideration. The young and old negroes are

[1] Jefferson gives notes of these remarks, p. 1102, *post.*
[2] Jefferson gives notes of these remarks, p. 1103, *post.*
[3] Jefferson gives notes of these remarks, p. 1099, *post.*

20719—VOL VI—06——15

a burthen to their owners. The eastern Colonies have a great advantage in trade. This will give them a superiority. We shall be governed by our interests, and ought to be. If I am satisfied in the rule of levying and appropriating money, I am willing the small Colonies should have a vote.[1]

Wilson. If the war continues two years, each soul will have forty dollars to pay of the public debt. It will be the greatest encouragement to continue slavekeeping, and to increase it, that can be, to exempt them from the numbers which are to vote and pay. Slaves are taxables in the Southern Colonies. It will be partial and unequal. Some Colonies have as many black as white; these will not pay more than half what they ought. Slaves prevent freemen from cultivating a country. It is attended with many inconveniences.[2]

Lynch. If it is debated, whether their slaves are their property, there is an end of the confederation. Our slaves being our property, why should they be taxed more than the land, sheep, cattle, horses, &c.?

Freemen cannot be got to work in our Colonies; it is not in the ability or inclination of freemen to do the work that the negroes do. Carolina has taxed their negroes; so have other Colonies their lands.

Dr. Franklin. Slaves rather weaken than strengthen the State, and there is therefore some difference between them and sheep; sheep will never make any insurrections.

Rutledge. I shall be happy to get rid of the idea of slavery. The slaves do not signify property; the old and young cannot work. The property of some Colonies is to be taxed, in others, not. The Eastern Colonies will become the carriers for the Southern; they will obtain wealth for which they will not be taxed.

AUGUST 1, 1776

Hooper. North Carolina is a striking exception to the general rule that was laid down yesterday, that the riches of a country are in proportion to the numbers of inhabitants. A gentleman of three or four hundred negroes don't raise more corn than feeds them. A laborer can't be hired for less than twenty-four pounds a year in Massachusetts Bay. The net profit of a negro is not more than five or six pounds per annum. I wish to see the day that slaves are not necessary.

[1] Jefferson gives remarks of John Adams and Benjamin Harrison, p. 1099, *post.*

[2] Jefferson's notes of Wilson's remarks are more full, and he adds some remarks by Robert Treat Paine and John Witherspoon. See p. 1101, *post.*

Whites and negroes cannot work together. Negroes are goods and chattels, are property. A negro works under the impulse of fear, has no care of his master's interest.[1]

The Consideration of the Seventeenth Article, resumed

Article 17. *Dr. Franklin* moves that votes should be in proportion to numbers. *Mr. Middleton* moves that the vote should be according to what they pay.

Sherman thinks we ought not to vote according to numbers. We are representatives of States, not individuals. States of Holland. The consent of everyone is necessary. Three Colonies would govern the whole, but would not have a majority of strength to carry those votes into execution. The vote should be taken two ways; call the Colonies, and call the individuals, and have a majority of both.

Dr. Rush.[2] Abbé Raynal has attributed the ruin of the United Provinces to three causes. The principal one is, that the consent of every State is necessary; the other, that the members are obliged to consult their constituents upon all occasions. We lose an equal representation; we represent the people. It will tend to keep up colonial distinctions. We are now a new nation. Our trade, language, customs, manners, don't differ more than they do in Great Britain. The more a man aims at serving America, the more he serves his Colony. It will promote factions in Congress and in the States; it will prevent the growth of freedom in America; we shall be loth to admit new Colonies into the confederation. If we vote by numbers, liberty will be always safe. Massachusetts is contiguous to two small Colonies, Rhode Island and New Hampshire; Pennsylvania is near New Jersey and Delaware; Virginia is between Maryland and North Carolina. We have been too free with the word independence; we are dependent on each other, not totally independent States. Montesquieu pronounces the confederation of Lycia, the best that ever was made; the cities had different weights in the scale. China is not larger than one of our Colonies; how populous! It is said that the small Colonies deposit their all; this is deceiving us with a word. I would not have it understood that I am pleading the cause of Pennsylvania; when I entered that door, I considered myself a citizen of America.

[1] Jefferson gives the vote on this article, p. 1102, *post*.
[2] Jefferson made more full notes of Rush's remarks, p. 1104, *post*.

for them, and to postpone the final decision to July 1. but that this might occasion as little delay as possible, a committee was appointed to prepare a declaration of independance. the commee were J. Adams, D[r] Franklin, Roger Sherman, Robert R. Livingston and myself. committees were also appointed at the same time to prepare a plan of confederation for the colonies, and to state the terms proper to be proposed for foreign alliance. the committee for drawing the declaration of independance desired me to do it. it was accordingly done, and being approved by them, I reported it to the house on Friday the 28th of June when it was read and ordered to lie on the table. On Monday the 1st of July the house resolved itself into a committee of the whole and resumed the consideration of the original motion made by the delegates of Virginia, which being again debated through the day, was carried in the affirmative by the votes of N. Hampshire, Connecticut, Massachusetts, Rhode island, N. Jersey, Maryland, Virginia, N. Carolina, and Georgia. S. Carolina and Pennsylvania voted against it. Delaware having but two members present they were divided: the delegates for N. York declared they were for it themselves, and were assured their constituents were for it, but that their instructions, having been drawn near a twelvemonth before, when reconciliation was still the general object, they were enjoined by them to do nothing which should impede that object. they therefore thought themselves not justifiable in voting on either side, and asked leave to withdraw from the question, which was given them. the comm͠ee rose and reported their resolution to the house. Mr Rutlege of S. Carolina then requested the determination might be put off to the next day, as he believed his collegues, tho they disapproved of the resolution, would then join in it for the sake of unanimity. the ultimate question whether the house would agree to the resolution of the comm͠ee, was accordingly postponed to the next day, when it was again moved and S. Carolina concurred in voting for it. in the mean time a third member had come post from the Delaware counties and turned the vote of that colony in favour of the resolution. members of a different sentiment attending that morning from Pennsylvania also, their vote was changed, so that the whole 12 colonies, who were authorized to vote at all, gave their voices for it; and within a few days the convention of N. York approved of it, and thus supplied the void occasioned by the withdrawing of their delegates from the vote.

Thomas Jefferson's Notes of Debates, July 1, 1776

Congress proceeded the same day to consider the declaration of Independance, which had been reported and laid on the table the Friday preceding, and on Monday referred to a commee of the whole. the pusillanimous idea that we had friends in England worth keeping terms with still haunted the minds of many. for this reason those passages which conveyed censures on the people of England were struck out lest they should give them offence. the clause too reprobating the enslaving the inhabitants of Africa was struck out in complaisance to S. Carolina and Georgia, who had never attempted to restrain the importation of slaves, and who on the contrary still wished to continue it. our Northern brethren also, I believe, felt a little tender under those censures; for tho' their people have very few slaves themselves, yet they had been pretty considerable carriers of them to others. the debates having taken up the greater parts of the 2d, 3d and 4th days of July, were, in the evening of the last, closed; the declaration was reported by the commee, agreed to by the house; and signed by every member[1] except mr Dickinson. as the sentiments of men are known not only by what they receive, but what they reject also, I will state the form of the declaration as originally reported. the parts struck out by Congress shall be distinguished by a black line drawn under them;[2] and those inserted by them shall be placed in the margin[3] or in a concurrent column.

A Declaration by the representatives of the United States of America in [**General**] *Congress assembled*

When in the course of human events it becomes necessary for one people to dissolve the political bands which have connected them with another, and to assume among the powers of the earth the separate and equal station, to which the laws of nature and of nature's god entitle them, a decent respect to the opinions of mankind requires that they should declare the causes which impel them to the separation.

We hold these truths to be self evident. that all men are created equal; that they are endowed by their creator with **certain** *inherent and* inalienable rights; that among these are life, liberty and the pursuit of happiness: that to secure these rights, governments are instituted among men, deriving their just powers from the consent of the governed; that whenever any form of govern-

[1] The original notes here insert the word "present."
[2] In the print these words are in italics.
[3] In the print these words are in black-face type.

he has abdicated government here **by declaring us out of his protection and waging war against us.** *withdrawing his governors and declaring us out of his allegiance and protection*

he has plundered our seas, ravaged our coasts, burnt our towns, and destroyed the lives of our people.

he is at this time transporting large armies of foreign mercenaries to compleat the works of death, desolation and tyranny already begun with circumstances of cruelty and perfidy **scarcely paralleled in the most barbarous ages, and totally** unworthy the head of a civilized nation.

he has constrained our fellow citizens taken captive on the high seas to bear arms against their country, to become the executioners of their friends and brethren, or to fall themselves by their hands.

Declaration of Independence debated, as reported in Jefferson's Notes of Debates, July 1-4, 1776. Words in italics are those struck out by Congress. Words in black-face type are those inserted by Congress

he has **excited domestic insurrections among us, and has** endeavored to bring on the inhabitants of our frontiers the merciless Indian savages, whose known rule of warfare is an undistinguished destruction of all ages, sexes and conditions *of existence.*

he has incited treasonable insurrections of our fellow-citizens with the allurements of forfeiture and confiscation of our property.

he has waged cruel war against human nature itself, violating it's most sacred rights of life and liberty in the persons of a distant people who never offended him, captivating and carrying them into slavery in another hemisphere, or to incur miserable death in their transportation thither. this piratical warfare, the opprobrium of infidel powers, is the warfare of the Christian king of Great Britain. determined to keep open a market where Men should be bought and sold, he has prostituted his negative for suppressing every legislative attempt to prohibit or to restrain this execrable commerce. and that this assemblage of horrors might want no fact of distinguished die, he is now exciting those very people to rise in arms among us, and to purchase that liberty of which he has deprived them, by murdering the people on whom he also obtruded them: thus paying off former crimes committed against the liberties of one people, with crimes which he urges them to commit against the lives of another.

In every stage of these oppressions we have petitioned for redress in the most humble terms: our repeated petitions have been answered only by repeated injuries. a prince whose char-

We therefore the representatives of the United states of America in General Congress assembled

do in the name and by authority of the good people of these *states reject and renounce all allegiance and subjection to the kings of Great Britain and all others who may hereafter claim by, through, or under them: we utterly dissolve all political connection which may heretofore have subsisted between us, and the people or parliament of Great Britain: and finally we do assert and declare these colonies to be free and independant states*

appealing to the supreme judge of the world for the rectitude of our intentions, do, in the name and by the authority of the good people of these colonies solemnly publish ~~and~~ declare that these United colonies are and of right ought to be free and independant states; that they are absolved from all allegiance to the British crown, and that all political connection between them and the state of Great Britain is and ought to be totally dissolved;

and that as free and independant states they have full power to levy war, conclude peace, contract alliances, establish commerce, and to do all other acts and things which independant states may of right do. and for the support of this declaration **with a firm reliance on the protection of divine providence** we mutually pledge to each other our lives, our fortunes and our sacred honor.

On Friday July 12. the committee appointed to draw the articles of Confederation reported them, and on the 22[d] the house resolved themselves into a commee to take them into consideration.[1] on the 30th and 31st of that month and 1st of the ensuing, those articles were debated which determined the proportion or quota of money which each state should furnish to the common treasury and the manner of voting in Congress. the first of these articles was expressed in the original draught in these words. 'Art. XI. all charges of war and all other expences that shall be incurred for the common defence, or general welfare, and allowed by the United states assembled, shall be defrayed out of a common treasury, which shall be supplied by the several colonies in proportion to the number of inhabitants of every age, sex and quality, except Indians not paying taxes in each colony,

Thomas Jefferson's Notes of Debates concerning Article XI of the Articles of Confederation, July 30–August 1, 1776

[1]Adams gives notes of a debate on July 25 and 26, on p. 1076, *ante*.

a true account of which, distinguishing the white inhabitants, shall be triennially taken and transmitted to the assembly of the United states.'

Mr Chase[1] moved that the quotas should be fixed, not by the number of inhabitants of every condition, but by that of the 'white inhabitants.' he admitted that taxation should be alwais in proportion to property; that this was in theory the true rule, but that from a variety of difficulties it was a rule which could never be adopted in practice. the value of the property in every state could never be estimated justly and equally. some other measure for the wealth of the state must therefore be devised, some standard referred to which would be more simple. he considered the number of inhabitants as a tolerably good criterion of property, and that this might alwais be obtained. he therefore thought it the best mode which we could adopt, with one exception only. he observed that negroes are property, and as such cannot be distinguished from the lands or personalties held in those states where there are few slaves. that the surplus of profit which a Northern farmer is able to lay by, he invests in cattle, horses &c. whereas a Southern farmer lays out that same surplus in slaves. there is no more reason therefore for taxing the Southern states on the farmer's head, and on his slave's head, than the Northern ones on their farmers' heads and the heads of their cattle. that the method proposed would therefore tax the Southern states according to their numbers and their wealth conjunctly, while the Northern would be taxed on numbers only: that negroes in fact should not be considered as members of the state, more than cattle, and that they have no more interest in it.

Mr John Adams observed that the numbers of people were taken by this article as an index of the wealth of the state and not as subjects of taxation. that as to this matter it was of no consequence by what name you called your people whether by that of freemen or of slaves. that in some countries the labouring poor were called freemen, in others they were called slaves: but that the difference as to the state was imaginary only. what matters it whether a landlord, employing ten laborers in his farm, gives them annually as much money as will buy them the necessaries of life, or gives them those necessaries at short hand. the ten labourers add as much wealth annually to the state, increase it's exports as much in the one case as the other. certainly 500 freemen produce no more profits, no greater surplus for

[1] Adams gives notes on this speech, and shows that it was made on July 30. See p. 1079, *ante*.

the paiment of taxes than 500 slaves. therefore the state in which are the labourers called freemen should be taxed no more than that in which are those called slaves. suppose by any extraordinary operation of nature or of law, one half the labourers of a state could in the course of one night be transformed into slaves: would the state be made the poorer or the less able to pay taxes? that the condition of the labouring poor in most countries, that of the fishermen particularly of the Northern states is as abject as that of slaves. it is the number of labourers which produce the surplus for taxation, and numbers therefore indiscriminately are the fair index of wealth. that it is the use of the word 'property' here, and it's application to some of the people of the state, which produces the fallacy. how does the Southern farmer procure slaves? either by importation or by purchase from his neighbor. if he imports a slave, he adds one to the number of labourers in his country, and proportionably to it's profits and abilities to pay taxes. if he buys from his neighbor, it is only a transfer of a labourer from one farm to another, which does not change the annual produce of the state, and therefore should not change it's tax. that if a Northern farmer works ten labourers on his farm, he can it is true, invest the surplus of ten mens' labour in cattle: but so may the Southern farmer working ten slaves. that a state of 100,000 freemen can maintain no more cattle than one of 100,000 slaves. therefore they have no more of that kind of property. that a slave may indeed from the custom of speech be more properly called the wealth of his master, than the free labourer might be called the wealth of his employer: but as to the state both were equally it's wealth, and should therefore equally add to the quota of it's tax.

Mr Harrison proposed a compromise, that two slaves should be counted as one freeman. he affirmed that slaves did not do so much work as freemen, and doubted if two effected more than one. that this was proved by the price of labor, the hire of a labourer in the Southern colonies being from 8. to 12 £, while in the Northern it was generally 24 £.

Mr Wilson said that if this amendment should take place the Southern colonies would have all the benefit of slaves, whilst the Northern ones would bear the burthen. that slaves increase the profits of a state, which the Southern states mean to take to themselves; that they also increase the burthen of defence, which would of course fall so much the heavier on the Northern. that slaves occupy the places of freemen and eat their food. dismiss your slaves and freemen will take their places. it is our duty to lay every discouragement on the importation of slaves: but this amendment would give the jus trium liberorum to him who would import slaves. that other kinds of property were pretty equally distributed thro' all the colonies: there were as many cattle, horses, and sheep in the North as the South, and South as the North: but not so as to slaves. that experience has shewn that those colonies have been alwais able to pay most which have the most inhabitants, whether they be black or white. and the practice of the Southern colonies has always been to make every farmer pay poll taxes upon all his labourers whether they be black or white. he acknowledges indeed that freemen work the most; but they consume the most also. they do not produce a greater surplus for taxation. the slave is neither fed nor clothed so expensively as a freeman. again white women are exempted from labour generally, which negro women are not. in this then the Southern states have an advantage as the article now stands. it has sometimes been said that slavery is necessary because the commodities they raise would be too dear for market if cultivated by freemen; but now it is said that the labour of the slave is the dearest.

Mr Payne urged the original resolution of Congress, to proportion the quotas of the states to the number of souls.

Dr Witherspoon was of opinion that the value of lands and houses was the best estimate of the wealth of a nation, and that it was practicable to obtain such a valuation. this is the true barometer of wealth. the one now proposed is imperfect in itself and unequal between the states. it has been objected that negroes eat the food of freemen, and therefore should be taxed. horses also eat the food of freemen; therefore they also should be taxed. it has been said too that in carrying slaves into the estimate of the taxes the state is to pay, we do no more than those states themselves do who always take slaves into the estimate of the taxes the individual is to pay. but the cases are not parallel. in the Southern colonies slaves pervade the whole colony; but they do not pervade the whole continent. that as to the original resolution of Congress,[1] it was temporary only, and related to the monies heretofore emitted: whereas we are now entering into a new compact and therefore stand on original ground.[2]

[1] The original notes here inserted, "to proportion the quotas according to the souls."

[2] Adams gives some remarks by Thomas Lynch, Benjamin Franklin, and Edward Rutledge. See p. 1080, *ante*. Also remarks on trade and the Indians.

the question being put, the amendment proposed was rejected by the votes of N. Hampshire, Massachusetts, Rhode island, Connecticut, N. York, N. Jersey, and Pennsylvania, against those of Delaware, Maryland, Virginia, North and South Carolina. Georgia was divided.

The other article was in these words.

'ART. XVII. In determining questions each colony shall have one vote.'

July 30. 31. Aug. 1. present 41 members. Mr Chase observed that this article was the most likely to divide us of any one proposed in the draught then under consideration. that the larger colonies had threatened they would not confederate at all if their weight in Congress should not be equal to the numbers of people they added to the confederacy; while the smaller ones declared against a union if they did not retain an equal vote for the protection of their rights. that it was of the utmost consequence to bring the parties together, as should we sever from each other, either no foreign power will ally with us at all, or the different states will form different alliances, and thus increase the horrors of those scenes of civil war and bloodshed which in such a state of separation and independance would render us a miserable people. that our importance, our interests, our peace required that we should confederate, and that mutual sacrifices should be made to effect a compromise of this difficult question. he was of opinion the smaller colonies would lose their rights, if they were not in some instances allowed an equal vote, and therefore that a discrimination should take place among the questions which would come before Congress. that the smaller states should be secured in all questions concerning life or liberty, and the greater ones in all respecting property. he therefore proposed that in votes relating to money, the voice of each colony should be proportioned to the number of it's inhabitants.

Dr Franklin thought that the votes should be so proportioned in all cases. he took notice that the Delaware counties had bound up their delegates to disagree to this article. he thought it a very extraordinary language to be held by any state, that they would not confederate with us unless we would let them dispose of our money. certainly if we vote equally we ought to pay equally: but the smaller states will hardly purchase the privilege at this price. that had he lived in a state where the representation, originally equal, had become unequal by time and accident, he might have submitted rather than disturb

requisite on all occasions. 2. their obligation to consult their constituents. 3. their voting by provinces. this last destroyed the equality of representation; and the liberties of Great Britain also are sinking from the same defect. that a part of our rights is deposited in the hands of our legislatures. there it was admitted there should be an equality of representation. another part of our rights is deposited in the hands of Congress: why is it not equally necessary there should be an equal representation there? were it possible to collect the whole body of the people together, they would determine the questions submitted to them, by their majority. why should not the same majority decide, when voting here by their representatives? the larger colonies are so providentially divided in situation as to render every fear of their combining, visionary. their interests are different, and their circumstances dissimilar. it is more probable they will become rivals and leave it in the power of the smaller states to give preponderance to any scale they please. the voting by the number of free inhabitants will have one excellent effect, that of inducing the colonies to discourage slavery and to encourage the increase of their free inhabitants.

Dr. Rush's reference to slavery in debate on Article XVII of Articles of Confederation, as reported in Thomas Jefferson's Notes of Debates, July 30-August 1, 1776

Mr. Hopkins observed there were 4. larger, 4 smaller and 4 middle-sized colonies. that the four largest would contain more than half the inhabitants of the Confederating states, and therefore would govern the others as they should please. that history affords no instance of such a thing as equal representation. the Germanic body votes by states. the Helvetic body does the same; and so does the Belgic confederacy. that too little is known of the antient confederations to say what was their practice.

Mr Wilson thought that taxation should be in proportion to wealth, but that representation should accord with the number of freemen. that government is a collection or result of the wills of all. that if any government could speak the will of all it would be perfect; and that so far as it departs from this it becomes imperfect. it has been said that Congress is a representation of states, not of individuals. I say that the objects of it's care are all the individuals of the states. it is strange that annexing the name of 'State' to ten thousand men, should give them an equal right with forty thousand. this must be the effect of magic, not of reason. as to those matters which are referred to Congress, we are not so many states; we are one large state. we lay aside our individuality whenever we come here. the

Consideration of the 14th Article of Confederation, line 47, October 30, 1777

It was then moved after "same" in the 47 l. to insert "provided that the nine states so assenting shall comprehend a majority of the people of the united states excluding negroes and indians, for which purpose a true account of the number of free people in each State shall be trienially taken and transmitted to the assembly of the united states." And the yeas and nays being required:

New Hampshire,		
Mr. Folsom,	no	no
Massachusetts Bay,		
Mr. S. Adams,	ay	no
J. Adams,	no	
Gerry,	no	
Lovell,	no	
Rhode Island,		
Mr. Marchant,	no	no
Connecticut,		
Mr. Dyer,	no	no
Law,	no	
Williams,	no	
New York,		
Mr. Duane,	no	no
Duer,	no	
New Jersey,		
Mr. Witherspoon,	no	no
Elmer,	no	
Pennsylvania,		
Mr. Roberdeau,	no	no
Maryland,		
Mr. Smith,	ay	*
Virginia,		
Mr. Jones,	ay	ay
R. H. Lee,	ay	
F. L. Lee,	ay	
Harvie,	ay	
North Carolina,		
Mr. Penn,	no	no
Harnett,	no	
South Carolina,		
Mr. Heyward,	no	no
Laurens,	no	

So it passed in the negative.

It was then moved after "kind" in the 8 l. to strike out "shall be capable of being a delegate."

And in the 6 l. after "person" to insert "being a delegate shall be capable of."

On the question put,

Resolved in the affirmative.

And the question being put on the several paragraphs as amended, the same were agreed to.

Deane and the other commissioners of the United States at the court of France.

Resolved, That Monday next be assigned for choosing a commissioner to the court of France, in place of Silas Deane, Esqr [1]

The committee to whom were referred the return of ordnance, &c. taken from the enemy, and the letter from the council of safety of New York, brought in a report, which was taken into consideration; and after debate,

Resolved, That the same be re-committed.

||The several matters to this day referred, being postponed,

Adjourned to 10 o'Clock to Morrow.|| [2]

[1] In the *Papers of the Continental Congress*, No. 19, III, folio 165 is a memorandum in the writing of Henry Laurens: "Nominations 21st Novr A. M. for a commissioner, the Court of France. Mr. Dana, Mr. Jas. Wilson, ~~Marquis de la Fayette, Col. R. H. Lee,~~ Mr. John Adams, Col. Jos. Reed.

Letter concerning debate on the Articles of Confederation, November 21, 1777. Mr. Folsom was a delegate to Congress from New Hampshire

[2] "Inclosed I send you a Copy of the Confederation, the Eighth article of which respects Taxation, and has given me great uneasiness, as I cannot see any Justice in the Rule therein laid down, for proportioning the several States with the charges of the present war. In the first place, it appears to me that one third part of the wealth of the Southern States which consists in Negroes, is entirely left out, and no notice taken of them in determining their ability to pay taxes, notwithstanding it is by them that they procure their wealth; neither are we to have any advantage of them in proportioning the number of men to be drawn from the several States to carry on the war, that being fixed on the number of white inhabitants in each State, so that by their negroes being left at home, they can till their lands and get bread and riches, while some other States may be greatly distressed. In the next place, the wealth that is in some States more than there is in others, by no means fixes a proportionable Value on the Lands in such States,—which if this be true, seems to prove that the plan laid down by Congress is not just: These are my own thoughts on this head; but refer you to your own better judgment on them. It seems to be the sense of Congress, that if any of the Articles of Confederation, should be thought hard of or unequal to any of the States, that they will make a representation of the same to Congress, with the reasons of their disapprobation to such articles, in order if possible to give satisfaction and ease to each and every of the States. The time fixed on for the several Legislatures, to determine on these great Points, is by some members thought too short; but I make no doubt but they will take as much time to deliberate thereon as may be thought just and necessary." *Nathaniel Folsom to Meshech Weare*, 21 November, 1777. *New Hampshire StatePapers*, VIII, 755.

to observe, that the present war, as we always apprehended, was undertaken for the general defence and interest of the confederating colonies, now the United States. It was ever the confident expectation of this State, that the benefits derived from a successful contest, were to be general and proportionate; and that the property of the common enemy, falling in consequence of a prosperous issue of the war, would belong to the United States, and be appropriated to their use. We are therefore greatly disappointed in finding no provision made in the confederation for empowering the Congress to dispose of such property, but especially the vacant and unpatented lands, commonly called the crown lands, for defraying the expences of the war, and for other such public and general purposes. The jurisdiction ought in every instance to belong to the respective states within the charter or determined limits of which such lands may be seated; but reason and justice must decide, that the property which existed in the crown of Great Britain, previous to the present revolution, ought now to belong to the Congress, in trust for the use and benefit of the United States. They have fought and bled for it, in proportion to their respective abilities, and therefore the reward ought not to be predilectionally distributed. Shall such states as are shut out by situation from availing themselves of the least advantage from this quarter, be left to sink under an enormous debt, whilst others are enabled, in a short period, to replace all their expenditures from the hard earnings of the whole confederacy?

7. The 9 article also provides, that the requisition for land forces to be furnished by the several states shall be proportioned to the number of *white* inhabitants in each. In the act of independence we find the following declaration: "We hold these truths to be self-evident, that all men are created equal; that they are endowed by their Creator with certain unalienable rights, among which are life, liberty, and the pursuit of happiness:" of this doctrine it is not a very remote consequence, that all the inhabitants of every society, be the colour of their complexion what it may, are bound to promote the interest thereof, according to their respective abilities. They ought therefore to be brought into the account on this occasion. But, admitting necessity or expediency to justify the refusal of liberty in certain circumstances to persons of a particular colour, we think it unequal to reckon nothing upon such in this case. Should it be improper, for special local reasons, to admit them in arms for the defence of the nation, yet we conceive the proportion of forces to be embodied ought to be fixed according to the whole number of inhabitants in the State,

Proposals from New Jersey concerning the Articles of Confederation, read June 25, 1778

from whatever class they may be raised. If the whole number of inhabitants in a State, whose inhabitants are all whites, both those who are called into the field, and those who remain to till the ground, and labour in mechanical arts and otherwise, are reckoned in the estimate for striking the proportion of forces to be furnished by that State, ought even a part of the latter description to be left out in another? As it is of indispensable necessity in every war, that a part of the inhabitants be employed for the uses of husbandry and otherwise at home, while others are called into the field, there must be the same propriety that persons of a different colour, who are employed for this purpose in one State, while *whites* are employed for the same purpose in another, be reckoned in the account of the inhabitants in the present instance.

8. In order that the quota of troops to be furnished in each State, on occasion of a war, may be equitably ascertained, we are of opinion that the inhabitants of the several states ought to be numbered as frequently as the nature of the case will admit, and once at least every five years. The disproportionate increase in the population of different states may render such provision absolutely necessary.

9. It is provided in the 9th article, that the assent of nine states out of thirteen shall be necessary to determine in sundry cases of the highest concern. If this proportion be proper and just, it ought to be kept up, should the states increase in number, and a declaration thereof be made, for the satisfaction of the Union.

That we think it our indispensable duty to solicit the attention of Congress to these considerations and remarks, and to request that the purport and meaning of them be adopted as part of the general confederation; by which means we apprehend the mutual interests of all the states will be better secured and promoted, and that the legislature of this State will then be justified in ratifying the same.

Whereupon, a motion was made,

That the several articles in the confederation, referred to in the representation of the State of New Jersey, be so far re-considered as to admit the purport and meaning of the additions, alterations, and amendments, proposed in the said representation:

Question put,

Passed in the negative, 3 ayes, 6 noes, one divided.

The delegates of Pennsylvania were then called on for the report of their constituents relative to the articles of confederation; Whereupon,

They moved in behalf of their State:

1. In the first paragraph of the 5th article, to expunge the words "for the remainder of the year:"

Question put,

Passed in the negative, 2 ayes, 8 noes, 1 divided.

2. That such part of the 9th article as respects the post office, be altered or amended, so as that Congress be obliged to lay the accounts annually before the legislature of the several states:

Question put,

Passed in the negative, 2 ayes, 9 noes.

3. In the 5th paragraph of the 9 article, to expunge the word "white:"

Question put,

Passed in the negative, 3 ayes, 7 noes, one divided.

Vote on New Jersey proposal on apportioning of troop quotas according to whole number of inhabitants of states, not just white inhabitants, as provided in the 9th Article of Confederation, June 25, 1778

4. In the last section of the 9th article, after the word "delegates," add "respectively:"

Question put,

Passed in the negative, 1 ay, 10 noes.

The delegates from Virginia being called on for the report of their constituents, relative to the articles of confederation, informed Congress,

That they are empowered to ratify the same as they now stand.

The delegates from South Carolina being called upon for the report of their constituents upon the confederation, moved in behalf of their State:

Motion and vote concerning the 4th Article of Confederation, June 25, 1778

1. In article 4th, between the words "free inhabitants," to insert "white:"

Passed in the negative, 2 ayes, 8 noes, 1 divided.

2. In the next line, after "these states," insert "those who refuse to take up arms in defence of the confederacy:"

Motion of South Carolina and vote concerning the 4th Article of Confederation, June 25, 1778

Passed in the negative, 3 ayes, 8 noes.

3. After the words "the several states," insert "according to the law of such states respectively, for the government of their own free white inhabitants:"

Passed in the negative, 2 ayes, 8 noes, 1 divided.

4. After the words "of which the owner is an inhabitant," insert "except in cases of embargo:"

Passed in the negative, 2 ayes, 9 noes.

5. In the 1 paragraph of 5 article, strike out "first Monday in November," and insert "nineteenth day of April:"

Passed in the negative, 1 ay, 9 noes, 1 divided.

6. In the 2 paragraph of 5 article, substitute "three," in place of "two," and "two" in place of "three," and "four" in place of "six:"

Passed in the negative, 2 ayes, 9 noes.

7. In 3 paragraph of 5 article, for "committee," read "grand council:"

Passed in the negative, 1 ay, 9 noes, 1 divided.

8. In the first paragraph of 6 article, for "prince or state," read "prince or foreign state, except the same be upon the subject of commerce, nor then so as to interfere with any treaty or alliance of the United States made or treaty proposed by Congress:"

Passed in the negative, 2 ayes, 9 noes.

9. In 2d paragraph of 6 article, strike out "by some nation of Indians," and after the words "to invade such state," insert "or upon requisition to assist a sister state actually invaded or threatened with an invasion:"

Passed in the negative, 3 ayes, 8 noes.

10. In 1 paragraph of 7 article, strike out the words "of or under the rank of colonel," and after "shall be appointed," insert "and commissioned:"

Passed in the negative, 2 ayes, 8 noes, 1 divided.

11. At the end of the 7 article add,

4. That the navigation of the river Mississippi, as low down as the southern boundary of the United States, be acknowledged and ratified absolutely free to the subjects of the United States.

Agreed

5. That free commerce be allowed to the subjects of the United States with some port or ports below the southern boundary of the said states, on the river Mississippi, except for such articles as may be particularly enumerated; and,

Rejected

6. In case the allies of these United States will agree to support them in such claim, by continuing hostilities, then to insist that Nova Scotia and its dependencies be ceded to the United States, or declared independent.

Rejected

On the second head, your committee are of opinion,

1. That the claim to Nova Scotia ought to be given up in lieu of the equal share in the Newfoundland fishery, or such share of the fishery in lieu of Nova Scotia, if both cannot be obtained.

Rejected

2. That in case neither of these can be obtained in lieu of the other, then, if the Bermuda Islands can be obtained, the claim to Nova Scotia be ceded in lieu thereof.

Rejected

3. That it may be stipulated, that the subjects of the United States shall not trade to the East Indies, or engage in the slave trade, if adequate compensation ~~therefore~~ can be obtained.

Agreed

Committee recommendations concerning instructions to be given to ministers negotiating a possible treaty with Spain, read February 23, 1779

4. That the United States will not establish any settlement, or dominion, beyond the limits of the said states, as settled at the conclusion of the treaty of peace.

Agreed

Congress judging it of the greatest importance to prescribe some invariable rules for the order and discipline of the troops, especially for the purpose of introducing an uniformity in their formation and manœuvres, and in the service of the camp:

Ordered, That the following regulations be observed by all the troops of the United States, and that all general and other officers cause the same to be executed with all possible exactness.

Ordered, That the Board of War cause as many copies thereof to be printed as they shall deem requisite for the use of the troops.

Committee report on defense of the southern states, read March 29, 1779

Congress resumed the consideration of the report of the committee on the circumstances of the southern states, and the ways and means for their safety and defence: wherein the committee report:

That the circumstances of the army will not admit of the detaching of any force for the defence of South Carolina and Georgia.

That the continental battalions of those two States are not adequate to their defence.

That the three battalions of North Carolina continental troops now on the southern service are composed of draughts from the militia for nine months only, which term with respect to a great part of them will expire before the end of the campaign.

That all the other force now employed for the defence of the said States consists of militia, who from the remoteness of their habitations and the difficulties attending their service ought not to be relied on for continued exertions and a protracted war.

That the State of South Carolina as represented by the delegates of the said State and by Mr. Huger, who has

51828—VOL XIII—08——25

come hither at the request of the governor of the said State, on purpose to explain the particular circumstances thereof, is unable to make any effectual efforts with militia, by reason of the great proportion of citizens necessary to remain at home to prevent insurrections among the negroes, and to prevent the desertion of them to the enemy.

That the state of the country and the great numbers of those people among them expose the inhabitants to great danger from the endeavours of the enemy to excite them, either to revolt or to desert. That it is suggested by the delegates of the said State, and by Mr. Huger, that a force might be raised in the said State from among the negroes which would not only be formidable to the enemy from their numbers and the discipline of which they would very readily admit, but would also lessen the danger from revolts and desertions by detaching the most vigorous and enterprizing from among the negroes. That as this measure may involve inconveniences peculiarly affecting the states of South Carolina and Georgia, the committee are of opinion that the same should be submitted to the governing powers of the said states, and if the said powers shall judge it expedient to raise such a force, that the United States ought to defray the expence thereof; Whereupon,

~~Resolved, That it be recommended to the Governing Powers of the States of South Carolina and Georgia, to consider of the Necessity, and Utility of arming [if they shall with Congress think it expedient to take measures for immediately]~~[1] ~~raising a force of —— able bodied Negroes, either for filling up the continental Battalions of those States, or for forming separate Corps, to be commanded by white Commissioned and NonCommissioned Officers, the commissioned officers to be appointed by the said governing Powers respectively, or for both purposes.~~

[1] The words in brackets are in the writing of John Jay.

Resolved, That it be recommended to the states of South Carolina and Georgia, if they shall think the same expedient, to take measures immediately for raising three thousand able bodied negroes.

That the said negroes be formed into separate corps as battalions, according to the arrangements adopted for the main army, to be commanded by white commissioned and non commissioned officers.

That the commissioned officers be appointed by the said states.

That the non commissioned officers may, if the said states respectively shall think proper, be taken from among the non commissioned officers and soldiers of the continental battalions of the said states respectively.

That the governors of the said states, together with the commanding officer of the southern army, be empowered to incorporate the several continental battalions of their states with each other respectively, agreeable to the arrangement of the army as established by the resolutions of May 27, 1778, and to appoint such of the supernumerary officers to command the said negroes as shall chuse to go into that service.[1]

Resolved, That congress will make provision for paying the proprietors of such negroes as shall be inlisted for the service of the United States during the war, a full compensation for the property at a rate not exceeding one thousand dollars for each active able bodied negro man of standard size, not exceeding thirty five years of age, who shall be so inlisted and pass muster.

That no pay or bounty be allowed to the said negroes, but that they be cloathed and subsisted at the expence of the United States.

[1] These five paragraphs were substituted for the one paragraph in the original report, in the writing of Gouverneur Morris. They are on folio 369.

That every negro who shall well and faithfully serve as a soldier to the end of the present war, and shall then return his arms, be emancipated and receive the sum of fifty dollars.

Resolved, That it be recommended to the states of Virginia and North Carolina respectively, to raise as many battalions of regular troops, for the particular defence of the southern states, as their respective circumstances will admit; such troops to be engaged only for one year, not to be compelled to serve on any enterprise, or on the defence of any post to the northward of Virginia; to be entitled to continental pay, cloathing and subsistence, and a bounty not exceeding 200 dollars for every non-commissioned officer and soldier.

Whereas the Bahama Islands are now garrisoned by and under the military government of the king of Great Britain, and the inhabitants of the said Islands have of late fitted out many privateers and armed vessels for cruizing on the coasts of these United States; and such privateers and armed vessels have actually captured divers vessels, the property of the citizens of these states, on the coast of South Carolina:

Resolved, That the resolution of Congress of the twenty-fourth day of July, 1776, so far as it relates to the said Bahama Islands, be repealed, and from and after the date of this resolution held void.[1]

Whereas John Laurens, Esq. who has heretofore acted aid de camp to the Commander in Chief, is desirous of repairing to South Carolina, with a design to assist in defence of the southern states:

Resolved, That a commission of lieutenant colonel be granted to the said John Laurens, Esq. ~~his rank to com-~~

[1]This report, in the writing of Thomas Burke, is in the *Papers of the Continental Congress*, No. 20, II, folio 365.

Virginia,			*North Carolina,*		
Mr. T. Adams,	no	no	Mr. Penn,	ay	ay
F. L. Lee,	no		Hill,	no	
M. Smith,	no		Burke,	ay	
R. H. Lee,	no		*South Carolina,*		
Griffin,	no		Mr. Laurens,	no	div.
Nelson,	no		Drayton,	ay	
			Georgia,		
			Mr. Langworthy,	ay	ay

So it passed in the negative.

On the question to agree to the substitute, resolved in the affirmative.

A motion was then made by   to strike out the words, "and that all proceedings," &c. to the end; and on the question, shall those words stand, passed in the negative.

On the question to agree to the resolution as amended: resolved in the affirmative.

Mr Burke, having in debate declared that the supreme executive Council of Pennsylvania had acted in a waspish, peevish and childish manner, was called to order and it was thereupon moved that the sense of the House should be taken whether the said declaration was consistent with order.[1]

And the President being of opinion that Mr Burk was in order, an appeal was made to the House.

Report from War Office April 3, 1779

WAR OFFICE, *April 1, 1779.*

The Board have considered the case of Mon^sr Galvan, referred to them by Congress, and beg leave to inform,

That Mr. Galvan is a Captain in a regiment in the service of his Most Christian Majesty serving in the West Indies. His Commission is dated the 12th June, 1778, and signed by Mon^sr De Sartine, Minister of Marine.

That he (Mr Galvan) has served in a regiment raised in the State of South Carolina on Continental establishment in quality of 2nd Lieutenant, but left the same on being sent by the government of that State to France on the errand of obtaining supplies.

[1] This motion, in the writing of Elbridge Gerry and moved by him, is in the *Papers of the Continental Congress*, No. 36, I, folio 17a. The date in the endorsement is illegible. The subsequent three lines are in the writing of John Jay.

51828—VOL XIII—08——27

That Monsr. Galvan is in the opinion of the Board a man of capacity, and well qualified to act in the character of a Sub Inspector: But as these Officers must be taken from the line and be of the rank of Lieutenant Colonels, and of whom there are a sufficient number, it seems impracticable to introduce him in that Station in this Quarter.

If the Battalions of Negroes are raised, there appears to be a necessity for a person of Monsr Galvan's abilities to act as inspector to these troops particularly, but subordinate to the Sub Inspector of the Department for the sake of uniformity in the discipline and service. But as the raising these corps depends upon contingencies, the Board cannot found a report with certainty on the subject, but have submitted to Congress the following resolution:

That the memorial of Monsr Galvan be transmitted to the Governor and Council of the State of South Carolina, who are hereby authorized to appoint, if they shall think proper, Mr Galvan to the Office of Sub Inspector to the Battalion of Negroes proposed to be raised in the Southern States, if that event should take place. If such appointment shall be made, Monsr Galvan to have ~~the brevet rank of Lieutenant Colonel in the army of the United States~~ such rank as the Governor and Council of South Carolina shall think most expedient for the service, and be subject to the orders of the Inspector General and the Sub Inspector of the Southern Army.

Frost,	no	McLene,	no
Lovell,	no	Van Dyke,	no
Holten,	no	Plater,	no
Ellery,	no	Paca,	no
Collins,	no	Henry,	no
Dyer,	no	T. Adams,	no
Spencer,	no	F. L. Lee,	no
Jay,	no	Smith,	no
Floyd,	no	Rd. H. Lee,	no
Lewis,	no	Nelson,	no
Witherspoon,	ay	Penn,	no
Fell,	no	Hill,	no
Armstrong,	no	Burke,	no
Shippen,	no	Drayton,	no
Searle,	no	Langworthy,	no [1]
Muhlenburg,	no		

Adjourned to 10 oClock on Monday.

[1] This report is in the *Papers of the Continental Congress*, No. 147, III, folio 169, and is endorsed "Disagreed to, April 3, 1779." No mention of it is found in the Journals. The vote was endorsed on the report by Charles Thomson.

That as Congress expect very salutary effects from the appointment of the said committee, therefore all further proceeding on Governor Clinton's letter be postponed until they report.[1]

Congress proceeded in the consideration of the report of the Board of Treasury relative to finance, and some time being spent therein,

Adjourned to 10 oClock to Morrow.

THURSDAY, JUNE 17, 1779

A letter, of this day, from Thomas Paine,[2] was read.

A memorial of Israel Morris was read:

Ordered, That it be referred to the Board of Treasury.

Consideration and vote on slave trade provision in treaty negotiations, June 17, 1779

Congress proceeded to the consideration of the report of the committee on the letters from A. Lee, Esq. and the communications from the Minister Plenipotentiary of France, and some time being spent thereon,

Congress proceeded in the consideration of the report on the communications of the Minister of France, &c. And the sixth article in the report, under the first head, being read, the same was set aside by the previous question.

The articles under the second head were then taken into consideration; and the first and second were set aside by the previous question.

The third article was then read; and a division being called for, the first clause, to wit: "That it may be stipulated, that the United States shall not trade to the "East Indies, if adequate compensation can be obtained," was set aside by the previous question.

[1] This report, in the writing of Daniel of St. Thomas Jenifer, is in the *Papers of the Continental Congress*, No. 20, I, folio 353.

[2] The letter of Paine is in the *Papers of the Continental Congress*, No. 55, folio 69.

On the second clause, viz. "or, engage in the slave "trade, if adequate compensation can be obtained," the previous question being moved, the yeas and nays thereon required by Mr. [John] Jay—

New Hampshire,		
Mr. Whipple,	ay	ay
Massachusetts Bay,		
Mr. Gerry,	no	
Lovell,	ay	ay
Holten,	ay	
Rhode Island,		
Mr. Ellery,	ay	
Marchant,	ay	ay
Collins,	ay	
Connecticut,		
Mr. Sherman,	ay	
Huntington,	ay	ay
Spencer,	ay	
New York,		
Mr. Jay,	no	
Duane,	ay	ay
Morris,	ay	
Lewis,	ay	
New Jersey,		
Mr. Scudder,	ay	ay
Fell,	ay	
Pennsylvania,		
Mr. Armstrong,	ay	
Shippen,	ay	ay
Muhlenberg,	ay	
M'Lene,	ay	
Delaware,		
Mr. Dickinson,	ay	ay
M'Kean,	ay	
Maryland,		
Mr. Henry,	ay	ay
Jenifer,	ay	
Virginia,		
Mr. Smith,	ay	
Griffin,	ay	ay
Fleming,	ay	
North Carolina,		
Mr. Penn,	ay	
Burke,	ay	ay
Sharpe,	ay	
South Carolina,		
Mr. Laurens,	ay	ay
Drayton,	ay	

So it was resolved in the affirmative, and the clause set aside.

The fourth, fifth and sixth articles were severally set aside by the previous question.

Resolved, That a cessation of hostilities during the negotations may be agreed to, but not without the consent or our ally, nor unless it shall be previously stipulated that all the forces of the enemy shall be immediately withdrawn from the United States.

Ordered, That the farther consideration of the report be postponed.

on board the said sloop for Bermuda, to take charge of a vessel which his owners had built there. Bad weather and contrary winds induced him to bear away for St. Eustatia, and in that course, on the 22d day of November, he fell in with an armed sloop of eight guns which gave him chase under English colours, and which he believed to be a British privateer. This induced him to throw over board a letter he had from his owners directed to a merchant in Bermuda, which he had orders to do, if closely pursued: When the privateer came up with him, she fired under French colours, upon which he immediately hove to, thinking her to belong to subjects of his most Christian Majesty. He was brought on board the privateer with his mate, a mariner and a passenger,[1] and carried to Basse terre in Guadaloupe; and there he and all his crew were thrown into goal, kept in the closest confinement, and his sloop was tried and condemned as lawful prize in the court of admiralty, and the vessel and cargo sold for the benefit of the captors.[2]

William Bingham, Esq. agent for the United States at Martinique, complained of this proceeding to the Count D'Arbaud, governor general of Basse terre, Guadaloupe, in a letter, dated, 8 December, 1778. The Governor in his answer, of the 18 of the same month, justifies the sentence of the court of admiralty, and alledges that the reasons on which the same was grounded, to wit, the throwing papers over board and having two blank passports, were sufficient.

Committee report concerning a situation described in a letter of July 6, 1779, from William Bingham, as read September 4, 1779

Secondly. Mr. Benjamin Putnam, a native and citizen of the State of Massachusetts bay, embarked on board an American privateer, which was captured by the enemy and carried into Antigua, where he and the rest of the crew were

[1] The original report continued: "where they were treated with great indignity and pillaged of all their money and wearing apparel."

[2] The original report contained the following: "He signed several papers in the French language, which he did not understand, being terrified thereto (as he alledges on oath) by threats of imprisonment, not knowing what he signed."

confined as prisoners of war. He made his escape from prison, and lay some time concealed in the town of St. John's, and at length, cut a sloop out of the harbour and in her arrived, with another American prisoner and thirteen negroes and sundry articles of cargo, at Point à Petre, Guadaloupe. A few days after his arrival there, the Governor of Antigua sent a flag of truce to reclaim the vessel, negroes, &c. in virtue of an agreement entered into between some of the French and British governors of the West India islands, stipulating that no privateer or armed vessel belonging to either government, committed to their care, should make any incursion or descent for the purposes of robbing, burning, plundering, or carrying off negro slaves, or other property, on pain that such vessel should have her commission vacated, the plundered effects restored and the penalty bond prosecuted. The Count d'Arbaud accordingly restored the prize and confined Mr. Putnam in close prison two weeks; but afterwards, upon the remonstrance of William Bingham, Esq. he sent Mr. Putnam and three of the negroes to him at Martinique. It appears that Mr. Putnam has addressed the Count d'Estaing on this transaction, who, in a letter to Mr. Putnam, dated on board the *Languedoc*, June 8, 1779, politely promises him that if he will solicit the King for restitution, he the Count will with great pleasure join in endeavouring to obtain it.

Upon the first case, as above stated, the committee are of opinion, that by a resolve of Congress the subjects of any of the United States have a right to trade with the inhabitants of Bermuda, and that by throwing any paper overboard, other than passports, bills of lading, invoices or other ship's papers, no forfeiture of vessel or cargo can legally ensue; and upon the whole, that there appears to them no sufficient grounds for the condemnation of the sloop *Kitty* and her cargo in the court of admiralty of Guadaloupe.

Committee recommendation concerning Massachusetts man involved with slaves in Antigua, September 4, 1779

Upon the second case, as above stated, the committee are of opinion "that by the resolves of Congress, and the law of nations, Benjamin Putnam and the other persons, who cut the vessel out of the harbour of St Johns in Antigua, and carried her and the negro slaves on board to Basse terre in Guadaloupe, had a right to them, and that no agreement between the governors of the French and British islands in such case as this could affect any other persons than the subjects of the contracting parties; which will appear evidently to be the meaning of the recited agreement itself, which is restrained to vessels belonging to either government committed to their care, and the penalty is the having their commissions vacated, the plundered effects restored and the penalty bond prosecuted, which is totally inapplicable to Americans or persons not belonging to their governments, and who had not obtained commissions from them or under their respective sovereigns; and of course that the releasing of this vessel and the negroes by the governor of Guadaloupe, and causing them to be delivered up to the governor of Antigua, was unwarrantable and inconsistent with treaties subsisting between his most Christian Majesty and these United States;" Whereupon,

Resolved, That a representation of the before mentioned cases be made to the Minister Plenipotentiary of his most Christian Majesty to these states, in order that redress and restitution may be made to the parties aggrieved, in such manner as may be consistent with justice and the laws of Nations.[1]

The committee to whom were referred letters from General Washington and Colonel Simms, brought in a report; Whereupon,

[1] The last paragraph is a substitute, in the writing of John Jay, the original deferring the question entirely to the "wisdom and justice" of the King. The report, in the writing of Thomas McKean, is in the *Papers of the Continental Congress*, No. 19, I, folio 341.

under him as surgeon to the transient sick, in case of misdemeanor, in order that they be tried for misconduct or neglect of duty by a garrison court martial.[1]

The committee, to whom was referred the motion of the delegates of Georgia; and

Committee report concerning use of Negro troops in Georgia and South Carolina, as read December 9, 1780

The Committee to whom was referred the Motion from the Delegates of Georgia, Beg leave to report

That the several acts of the 29th of March 1779, recommending the Levy of Blacks for the defence of Georgia and South Carolina, were never received by the Legislature of the former, and consequently, could not be carried into execution by that State. That although the measure was not adopted in South Carolina at that time, the necessity of the present juncture, and the difficulty of compleating the Continental quotas of those States in the ordinary method makes it incumbent on them to employ this resource for their own and the general Interest.

Your Committee therefore submit the following Resolutions viz.

Resolved, That an officer be appointed to levy a Corps of one thousand able bodied negroes in Georgia and South Carolina, under the authority of the Executives of those States and that the said Executives be requested to give every possible support to the measure.

Resolved, That the said Corps be officered and organized under the directions of the Commanding officer in the Southern Department, who is to give every necessary assistance in procuring the said Levies.

That the officers be taken from such as may be spared from the Continental Line in the first instance and then from reduced officers, the preference being given to those of Georgia and South Carolina in proportion to the number of Levies obtained which officers are to be entitled to the same pay and Emoluments as other officers of equal rank in the Continental army.

Resolved, That the conditions offered to the Black Soldiers, be the same as expressed in the act of the 29th of March 1779, and that Congress will make provision for paying a reasonable price to the proprietors of such negroes, provided they be not adherents to the Enemy.

[1] This motion, in the writing of Theodorick Bland, is in the *Papers of the Continental Congress,* No. 36, IV, folio 435.

Resolved, That the Board of War be directed as soon as possible to procure and send forward a sufficient number of arms and accoutrements together with the necessary cloathing for the said Corps.[1]

The committee, to whom were referred the letters, of November 9 and December 6, from William Palfrey, delivered in their reports, which were read.

Congress took into consideration the report on Mr. Palfrey's letters and agreed to a draught of a commission and instructions to W. Palfrey as consul of these United States in France:

The Congress of the United States of North America to William Palfrey, Esquire, Greeting.

We, reposing special trust and confidence in your abilities and integrity, do by these presents constitute you our consul in France, during our pleasure, to exercise the functions, and to enjoy all the honours, authorities, pre-eminences, privileges, exemptions, rights and emoluments to the said office appertaining.[2]

And we do hereby enjoin it upon all merchants of these United States, and upon all captains, masters and commanders of ships and other vessels, armed or unarmed, sailing under our flag, as well as all others of our citizens, to acknowledge the said William Palfrey, and to obey him in his consular quality; praying and requesting our very dear great friend and ally his Most Christian Majesty, his governours and other officers whom it may concern, to permit the said William Palfrey[3] fully and peaceably to enjoy the said office, without giving or suffering to be given any molesta-

[1] This report, in the writing of John Sullivan, is in the *Papers of the Continental Congress*, No. 20, II, folio 443. It is indorsed by Thomson: "August 24, 1781, not to be acted upon."

[2] After the words "Consul in France," the committee report had these words: "with power to appoint Vice Consuls in such places there as you shall judge necessary," which are marked "postponed."

[3] The report adds: "and the Vice Consuls whom he may appoint."

All controversies concerning the private right of soil claimed under different grants of two or more states, whose jurisdictions as they may respect such lands, and the states which passed such grants are adjusted, the said grants or either of them being at the same time claimed to have originated antecedent to such settlement of jurisdiction, shall on the petition of either party to the congress of the united states, be finally determined as near as may be in the same manner as is before prescribed for deciding disputes respecting territorial jurisdiction between different states.

The united states in congress assembled shall also have the sole and exclusive right and power of regulating the alloy and value of coin struck by their own authority, or by that of the respective states—fixing the standard of weights and measures throughout the united states—regulating the trade and managing all affairs with the Indians, not members of any of the states, provided that the legislative right of any state within its own limits be not infringed or violated—establishing or regulating post-offices from one state to another, throughout all the united states, and exacting such postage on the papers passing thro' the same as may be requisite to defray the expences of the said office—appointing all officers of the land forces, in the service of the united states, excepting regimental officers—appointing all the officers of the naval forces, and commissioning all officers whatever in the service of the united states—making rules for the government and regulation of the said land and naval forces, and directing their operations.

The united states in congress assembled shall have authority to appoint a committee, to sit in the recess of congress, to be denominated "A Committee of the States," and to consist of one delegate from each state; and to appoint such other committees and civil officers as may be necessary for managing the general affairs of the united states under their direction—to appoint one of their number to preside, provided that no person be allowed to serve in the office of president more than one year in any term of three years; to ascertain the necessary sums of Money to be raised for the service of the united states, and to appropriate and apply the same for defraying the public expences—to borrow money, or emit bills on the credit of the united states, transmitting every half year to the respective states an account of the sums of money so borrowed or emitted,—to build and equip a navy—to agree upon the number of land forces, and to make requisitions from each state for its quota, in proportion to

Reference to assessing of troop quotas in proportion to white inhabitants, in Article IX of Articles of Confederation, as ratified March 1, 1781

the number of white inhabitants in such state; which requisition shall be binding, and thereupon the legislature of each state shall appoint the regimental officers, raise the men and cloath, arm and equip them in a soldier like manner, at the expence of the united states; and the officers and men so cloathed, armed and equipped shall march to the place appointed, and within the time agreed on by the united states in congress assembled: But if the united states in congress assembled shall, on consideration of circumstances judge proper that any state should not raise men, or should raise a smaller number than its quota, and that any other state should raise a greater number of men than the quota thereof, such extra number shall be raised, officered, cloathed, armed and equipped in the same manner as the quota of such state, unless the legislature of such state shall judge that such extra number cannot be safely spared out of the same, in which case they shall raise officer, cloath, arm and equip as many of such extra number as they judge can be safely spared. And the officers and men so cloathed, armed and equipped, shall march to the place appointed, and within the time agreed on by the united states in congress assembled.

The united states in congress assembled shall never engage in a war, nor grant letters of marque and reprisal in time of peace, nor enter into any treaties or alliances, nor coin money, nor regulate the value thereof, nor ascertain the sums and expences necessary for the defence and welfare of the united states, or any of them, nor emit bills, nor borrow money on the credit of the united states, nor appropriate money, nor agree upon the number of vessels of war, to be built or purchased, or the number of land or sea forces to be raised, nor appoint a commander in chief of the army or navy, unless nine states assent to the same: nor shall a question on any other point, except for adjourning from day to day be determined, unless by the votes of a majority of the united states in congress assembled.

The congress of the united states shall have power to adjourn to any time within the year, and to any place within the united states, so that no period of adjournment be for a longer duration than the space of six Months, and shall publish the Journal of their proceedings monthly, except such parts thereof relating to treaties, alliances or military operations, as in their judgment require secrecy; and the yeas and nays of the delegates of each state on any question shall be entered on the Journal, when it is desired by any delegate; and the delegates of a state, or any of them, at his or their request shall

Provision of ordinance about captures on water, as read in a committee report August 14, 1781

Passed Septem[r] 17th, 1781.

The ships and effects of a Citizen of the United States, or a Subject of ~~an ally of the U. S.~~ any foreign State other than an enemy retaken from a pirate and reclaimed by the owner, within a year and a day from the date of the sentence of condemnation, by a petition to the Court which shall have condemned the same, shall be restored to such owner, upon the payment of one third of the value of the ships and effects to the recaptor. Where no claim shall be put in within a year and a day, the whole value shall be adjudged to the recaptor.[1]

P.

On recaptures of a vessel under the protection of ~~an hostile~~ a vessel [belonging to an enemy] equipped in a warlike manner, or where the vessel retaken is so equipped the proportion to be withdrawn from the original owner shall be divided as in the case of a capture of an ~~hostile~~ [enemy's] vessel, equipped in a warlike manner.

On recaptures of a vessel, under the protection of an hostile vessel, not equipped in a warlike manner, and where the vessel retaken is not so equipped, the proportion to be withdrawn from the original owner shall be divided, as in the case of a capture of an hostile vessel, not equipped in a warlike manner.

~~On recaptures by a british crew; the whole of the proportion to be withdrawn from the original owner shall be divided, as in the case of a capture by a british crew.~~

~~No part shall be deducted from the proportion, withdrawn from the original owner, where the recapture shall have been made by a vessel fitted out at private expence.~~

[Recommitted.]

~~Upon the capture of a slave belonging to the enemy, he shall be forthwith emancipated~~

[Recommitted; reported again.]

Upon the recapture of a slave, [negro or mulatto] belonging to a citizen of one of the United States, ~~in which that property is yet tolerated,~~ the same rules shall be observed, as in the recapture of vessels.

The rules of decision in the several courts shall be the resolutions and ordinances of Congress, public treaties, when declared to be so by an Act of Congress, and the law of nations, according to the general usages of Europe. Public treaties shall have the preeminence in all trials.

[1] This paragraph, in the writing of Edmund Randolph, is in the *Papers of the Continental Congress*, No. 59, III, folio 304.

This act shall commence in force on the day of next.[1]

[1] This report, in the writing of Edmund Randolph, except the portions in brackets which are in Thomas McKean's writing, is in the *Papers of the Continental Congress*, No. 59, III, folios 297–300, 285, 291. It was made from the following draft:

In pursuance of the power delegated to Congress by the Confederation, in cases of capture on water

Be it ~~enacted~~ ordained by the United States in Congress assembled, that from and after the day of next, all resolutions of Congress relating to captures on water and coming within the purview of this ordinance, shall be null and void. But ~~until that day all~~ questions of this sort arising before that day shall be determined at any time during the present war with G. B. according to them in the same manner, as if this ordinance had never been made.

It shall be lawful to capture and ~~make prize~~ to obtain condemnation of the ~~moveable~~ property herein after enumerated; if found on the high seas, or between high and low water mark: that is to say:

1. All ships and other vessels of whatsoever size or denomination, belonging to ~~the king of Great Britain, or any subject of the said king,~~ any power or subject of a power; being an Enemy of the United States of America with their rigging, tackle, apparel and furniture;

2. All goods, wares and merchandizes, slaves being always particularly included in these terms; belonging to ~~the said king, or any of his subjects,~~ any power or subject of a power, being an enemy of the United States of America, borne and found in ~~a British~~ the bottom or vessel of ~~an~~ such enemy and all contraband &c: borne &c. on board of any ships or vessels, belonging to a neutral nation.

3. All Contraband goods, wares and merchandizes, belonging to an allied or neutral power ~~to Wit, (here insert from the Treaty with France,) which, according to the law of nations as received among the usages of Europe; are justly denominated contraband, and found in the bottom or vessel of an enemy:~~

In this description a slave belonging to a neutral power or its subjects actually employed in navigating a vessel authorized to make seizures, shall be included:

4. All vessels, goods, wares, and merchandizes, taken by virtue of letters of marque or reprisal.

5. All vessels, belonging to an ally of the United States if employed in carrying contraband goods, wares or merchandize, or soldiers to the enemy of the United States.

The following Captures shall not be lawful, viz:—

1. of hostile property found in neutral bottoms: contraband goods being always excepted.

2. of hostile property under the protection of neutral ~~coasts,~~ nations or princes.

3. of allied or neutral property found in the ship or vessel of an enemy of the United States, contraband property being excepted as aforesaid.

4. of the property of an ally of the enemy unless contraband or found in the bottom of the enemy; without a special act of Congress to that effect.

5. Qu: if some exception ought not to be made in favor of a Bermudian bringing salt only.

No prince, nor other State, nor any subject of the same shall be adjudged an enemy, until by some act of Congress shall be made declaratory thereof. The goods, wares,

The Committee to whom the Resolution relative to supplying the Governor of Virginia with passports for the importation of salt, was referred Report.

That it appears to your Committee that the command which the enemy have of the Sea Coast of Virginia, and the navigable waters thereof, wholly obstructs the importation and manufacture of salt, and their late ravages ~~through the country~~ have reduced the shipping to the lowest state, banished the seamen and destroyed all the salt that fell into their hands.

That a supply of this commodity is absolutely and essentially necessary for that State, as the army there, without salt meat, must experience the greatest sufferings.

FOOTNOTE—Continued.

~~use,~~ captors: if by a body or detachment of regular soldiers or militia for other purposes upon regular duty ~~in arms under authority~~ the whole shall be adjudged to the Captors to be divided in the following manner [deest] if by Militia not in arms under authority or citizens not liable to Militia duty, $\frac{1}{2}$ to the ~~United States~~ State to which they belong; the other to them, to be divided in the following manner: to wit: [deest]

~~Upon the capture of a vessel not equipped in a warlike manner, $\frac{1}{3}$ shall be always deducted for the use of the United States, where made by a vessel of war belonging to them, by regular soldiers or by militia in arms under authority; and for the use of any individual State, to which a vessel, militia not in arms under authority, or citizens not liable to militia duty making the capture may belong. The balance shall be decreed to the captors, to be divided in the proportions aforesaid according to the case. A third shall not be deducted, where the capture shall have been made by a vessel fitted out at private expence.~~

On recaptures of vessels under the protection [of] an hostile vessel equipped in a warlike manner or where the vessel retaken is so equipped the proportion to be ~~deducted~~ withdrawn from the original owner shall be divided, as in the case of a capture of an hostile vessel, equipped in a warlike manner.

Qu: if not best to give the whole of recaptures to the recaptors.

On recaptures made from an hostile vessel not equipped in a warlike manner, or where the vessel retaken shall not be so equipped, the said proportions shall be divided as in the case of a capture of an hostile vessel not equipped in a warlike manner.

But a third or any part shall not be deducted where the capture or recapture shall have been made by a vessel, fitted out at private expence and bearing a commission.

British Crew.

Mem: in case of Omission a general reference to be made for the rule of decision established in the Court-law, and to the law of Nations.

Make a clause as to Slaves.

This draft, in the writing of Edmund Randolph, is in the *Papers of the Continental Congress*, No. 59, III, folio 301. The following on folio 287 is in James Duane's writing:

General Law respecting property.

Negroes Mulattos or others whose services shall be claimed by an Enemy shall be emancipated.

But if the service of such negro, mulatto or other person captivated as aforesaid shall not be legally claimed by a citizen of these United States he shall be set at liberty.

86382°—VOL 21—12——7

List of reports not to be acted upon, as reported August 23, 1781

That the following reports of Special Committees to wit
The report relative to

	Bearing date.
An Inquiry into the conduct of James Anderson for selling public hemp	25 Nov. 1779
A plan of conducting commercial affairs	29 Nov. 1779
Arranging reports	9 May 1780
General Greene as quarter master general	26 July 1780
Bills to be furnished to Governor Rutledge	21 Aug. 1780
The privileges of members of Congress	24 Aug. 1780
A vessel belonging to Chas. Crowly lost in public service	10 Nov. 1780
Continuing loan offices	15 Nov. 1780
The memorial of New Jersey	24 Nov. 1780
Supplies to the French fleet and army	24 Nov. 1780
Taking off the embargo	6 Dec. 1780
Raising regiments of negroes in South Carolina and Georgia	8 Dec. 1780
Ordering flour from the magazines in Connecticut	22 Dec. 1780
The resignation of Adjutant General Scammell	29 Dec. 1780
The recall of Dr Franklin	28 Dec. 1780
Specie for the use of prisoners	3 Feby. 1781
Mr Laurens's confinement	2 Mar. 1781
Provisions to be sent to Fort Pitt	2 Mar. 1781
Removal of the German Prisoners	9 Mar. 1781
Furnishing money to Dr Binney	14 Mar. 1781
Expences of General McDougall in attending on Congress	15 Sept. 1780
Payment of interest on issuing the bills of credit of 18th March 1780	2 April 1780
Employment of the navy	29 June 1781
Provisions on Hudson's River	21 May 1781
Rank of Captain Jones and Captain Nicholson	29 June 1781

Ought not to be acted upon.

That the Reports relative to

	Bearing date.
A Court of inquiry on General Howe; committed	May 1780
Detention of the produce of the sales of the *Nostra Señiora's* cargo; committed	12 July 1780
American seamen whom the British refuse to exchange	7 Oct. 1780
Money requested by General Lee	3 Oct. 1780

the United States, so effectually as that one cannot attempt to enter into such port or place without evident danger.

All ships or other vessels, with their rigging, tackle, apparel and furniture, and with their cargoes, found in the possession of pirates.

The goods, wares and merchandizes to be adjudged contraband, are the following, that is to say,

Cannons, mortars, fire-arms, pistols, bombs, granadoes, bullets, balls, fuses, flints, matches, powder, salt-petre, sulphur, carcases, pikes, swords, belts, pouches, cartouch-boxes, saddles and bridles, in any quantity beyond what may be necessary for the ship's provision, and may properly appertain to, and be adjudged necessary for, every man of the ship's crew or for each passenger.

If it shall manifestly appear, that of any entire thing of which division cannot be made without injury to its value, a subject of the enemy, and a citizen or a subject of a foreign power, not being an enemy, are joint holders, the whole shall be condemned and sold for gold or silver, the proper proportion of the net proceeds of which shall be deposited in the treasury of the State in which the sale shall be, to be paid to the order of such citizen, or the subject of such foreign power.

If such division can be accomplished, but neither the citizen nor the subject of a foreign power, nor his agent, shall require specific restitution of his property, there shall be a sale in the same manner as if the property were indivisible. But if in such case a requisition be made to this effect, the due proportion shall be specifically restored.

Where property shall have been originally captured on land from a State, or a citizen of the United States, and shall be re-captured below high-water mark by another citizen thereof, restitution shall be made to the former owner upon the payment of a reasonable salvage, not exceeding one-fourth part of the value; no regard being had to the time of possession by the enemy.

In all cases of re-capture by an armed vessel, fitted out at the expence of the United States, of a vessel or other effects belonging to a citizen, the court shall adjudge the proportion which would be due to the United States to be remitted to such citizen, no regard being had to the time of possession by the enemy.

On the re-capture by a citizen of any negro, mulatto, Indian, or other person, from whom labour or service is lawfully claimed by a State or a citizen of a State, specific restitution shall be adjudged to the claimant, whether the original capture shall have been made

Third reading and passage of ordinance concerning sea captures, December 4, 1781

on land or water, and without regard to the time of possession by the enemy, a reasonable salvage being paid by the claimant to the re-captor, not exceeding one-fourth of the value of such labour or service, to be estimated according to the laws of the State ~~of which the claimant shall be a citizen~~ under which the claim shall be made

But if the service of such negro, mulatto, Indian, or other person, captured below high-water mark, shall not be legally claimed ~~by a citizen of these United States~~ within a year and a day from the sentence of the court, he shall be set at liberty.

In all other cases of re-capture, restitution shall be made to the owner upon payment of one-third part of the true value for salvage, if the property shall have been re-taken in less than twenty-four hours after the capture. But if it shall not have been re-taken until the expiration of twenty-four hours after the capture, restitution shall not be made of any part.

Besides those who are duly authorised to make captures by special commission, captures of the property of an enemy shall be adjudged lawful when made:

1st. By a private vessel not having such commission, satisfactory proof being produced that they were made in pursuing the course of her voyage, and repelling a previous attack from an enemy.

2d. By any body or detachment of regular soldiers.

3d. By inhabitants of the country, if made within cannon-shot of the shore.

4th. By an armed vessel sailing under a commission of his Most Christian Majesty.

5th. By the crews of British vessels, while captures of this sort are licensed by the British.

Re-captures shall be made by no other persons than those authorised to make captures, except the crews of vessels re-taken.

The destruction of papers, or the possession of double papers by any captured vessel, shall be considered as evidence for condemnation, unless good cause be shewn to the contrary.

From and after the first day of ~~November~~ February, which shall be in the year of our Lord ~~1781~~ one thousand seven hundred and eighty-two, any letters of passport or safe conduct, granted before the 27th of March last, under the authority of Congress, to any person whatsoever, for removal of property from a place beyond sea within the dominions or possessions of the British king, shall be void.

Upon the capture of a vessel commissioned as a man of war or privateer, by any of the vessels of war of the United States of America,

ments for a permanent naval force, and it will always be least objectionable to borrow for that purpose on funds already established.

The requisition of a five per cent impost made on the 3rd day of February 1781, has not yet been complied with by the State of Rhode Island; but as there is reason to believe that their compliance is not far off, this Revenue may be considered as being already granted. It will however be very inadequate to the purposes intended. If goods be imported and prizes introduced to the amount of twelve millions annually, the five per cent would be six hundred thousand, from which at least one sixth must be deducted as well for the cost of collection, as for the various defalcations, which will necessarily happen, and which it is unnecessary to enumerate. It is not safe therefore to estimate this Revenue at more than half a million of dollars, for tho' it may produce more, yet probably it will not produce so much. It was in consequence of this, that on the 27th day of February last I took the liberty to submit the propriety of asking the States for a Land Tax of one dollar for every hundred acres of land, a Poll Tax of one dollar on all freemen, and all male slaves between 16 and 60 (excepting such as are in the federal army, and such as are by wounds or otherwise rendered unfit for service) and an excise of one eighth of dollar per gallon, on all distilled spirituous liquors. Each of these may be estimated at half a million, and should the product be equal to the estimation, the sum total of Revenues for funding the public Debts would be equal to two millions. What has been the fate of these propositions I know not; but I will beg leave on this occasion, not only to renew them but also to state some reasons in their favor and answer some objections against them.

Letter of July 29, 1782, from Superintendent of Finance, referred to committee, August 5, 1782

And first, as to a Land Tax. The advantages of it are, that it can be reduced to a certainty as to the amount and time. That no extraordinary means are necessary to ascertain it. And that land being the Ultimate object of human avarice, and that particular species of permanent property which so peculiarly belongs to a Country as neither to be removed nor concealed, it stands foremost for the object of taxation and ought most particularly to be burthened with those Debts which have been incurred by defending the freedom of its Inhabitants. But besides these general reasons, there are some which are in a manner peculiar to this Country; the land of America may, as to the proprietors be divided into two kinds, that which belongs to the great Landholder and that which is owned and occupied by the industrious cultivator. This latter class of citizens is generally speaking the most numerous and most valuable part of a

War to inform Captain Carnes that his farther attendance on this business can be dispensed with.[1]

Ordered, That the Secretary at War forward to the Commander in Chief a copy of Major General Greene's letter on the subject; and that he inform Captain Carnes that his farther attendance on this business can be dispensed with.

On motion of Mr. [James] Madison, seconded by Mr. [Arthur] Lee,[2]

Resolutions and votes, September 10, 1782

Resolved, That the Secretary for Foreign Affairs be and he is hereby directed to obtain as speedily as possible authentic returns of the slaves and other property ~~capable of being identified~~ which have been carried off or destroyed in the course of the war by the enemy, and to transmit the same to the ministers plenipotentiary for negociating a peace.[3]

On the question to agree to this, the yeas and nays being required by Mr. [Turbett] Wright,

State	Member	Vote	State vote
New Hampshire,			
	Mr. Gilman,	no	*
Massachusetts,			
	Mr. Osgood,	ay	ay
	Jackson,	ay	
Rhode Island,			
	Mr. Cornell,	ay	div.
	Howell,	no	
Connecticut,			
	Mr. Huntington,	ay	ay
	Dyer,	ay	
New York,			
	Mr. Duane,	ay	ay
	L'Hommedieu,	ay	
New Jersey,			
	Mr. Clark,	no	no
	Condict,	no	
	Witherspoon,	ay	
Pennsylvania,			
	Mr. Montgomery,	ay	ay
	Smith,	ay	
	Clymer,	ay	
	Atlee,	ay	
Delaware,			
	Mr. McKean,	ay	ay
	Wharton,	ay	

[1] This report is in the *Papers of the Continental Congress,* No. 149, I, folio 675.

[2] Madison's motion and the vote and resolution following it, in regard to confiscated property, were also entered in the manuscript Secret Journal, Foreign Affairs. The motion and the resolution were also entered in Secret Journal, No. 4.

[3] This resolution, in the writing of James Madison, is in the *Papers of the Continental Congress,* No. 36, I, folio 379. The vote is indorsed on it.

Maryland,		
Mr. Hanson,	no	
Carroll,	no	no
Wright,	no	
Virginia,		
Mr. J. Jones,	ay	
Madison,	ay	ay
Bland,	ay	
Lee,	ay	
North Carolina,		
Mr. Williamson,	ay	ay
Blount,	ay	
South Carolina,		
Mr. Rutledge,	ay	
Ramsay,	ay	
Izard,	ay	ay
Gervais,	ay	
Middleton,	ay	
Georgia,		
Mr. Telfair,	ay	
N. W. Jones,	ay	ay
Few,	ay	

So it was resolved in the affirmative.

Resolved, That in the meantime the Secretary for Foreign Affairs inform the said ministers that ~~great numbers~~ many thousand of slaves and ~~such~~ other property ~~as aforesaid~~ to a very great amount have been carried off or destroyed by the enemy.

~~That the said ministers be instructed in case any stipulations should become unavoidable in a treaty of peace in favor of a restitution of property confiscated within the United States to contend in the most earnest manner for a restitution to the citizens of the United States of such slaves and other property as aforesaid, as shall appear to have been plundered from them by the Enemy or their adherents.~~[1]

And that in the opinion of Congress the great loss of property which the citizens of the United States have sustained by the enemy will be considered by the several states as an insuperable bar to their making restitution or indemnification to the former owners of property which has been or may be forfeited to or confiscated by any of the states.[2]

On motion of Mr. [Thomas] Smith, seconded by Mr. [Eliphalet] Dyer,

[1] These resolutions, in the writing of James Madison, are in the *Papers of the Continental Congress*, No. 36, I, folio 379.

[2] This resolution, in the writing of John Rutledge, is in the *Papers of the Continental Congress*, No. 36, I, folio 377.

the committee are of opinion, that it is expedient to remit in favor of the original owners, the property re-captured by Colonel Kosciuszko, and retained for the use of the United States.

Upon this view of the subject, the committee propose the following resolutions:

1. That Congress approve of the steps taken by Major General Greene, in the case of the property re-captured on land by Colonel Kosciuszko, and claimed in behalf of the original owners, by the executive authority of the State of South Carolina, as stated in his letter of the 28 of October last:

2. That so much of the property re-captured as aforesaid, and accruing to the use of the United States, as shall be satisfactorily proven to have been captured from the inhabitants of the United States, be remitted to the original proprietors, excepting only so much, or the value thereof, not exceeding one fourth of the whole value, as the said Major General Greene may have promised, or may be deemed by him a proper compensation to the re-captors:

3. That leave be given to the committee to report an ordinance declaring in all cases what captures on land shall be legal, and in what manner the same shall be divided or appropriated.

Negatived.

~~That until such general provision shall be made, all property, dead victuals and provender of all kinds being excepted, which shall be recaptured on land from the enemy by forces in the service of the U. States and which shall be satisfactorily proven to have been previously captured from any individual State or without collusion captured or plundered from any inhabitant of the United States which shall be specifically restored to such State or to such inhabitant, on their paying therefor such sum not exceeding ¼ of its value, as may have been promised by the Commanding Officer of the Department to the recaptors, or as may be deemed by him a proper compensation to them; provided always that where slaves shall be so re-captured restitution shall be made without demand of such sum from the original owners, and provided that this~~

Resolutions proposed December 23, 1782

~~resolution shall not be construed to extend to property brought off from the enemy by deserters.~~[1]

The question being taken on the first resolution, resolved in the affirmative.

When the second was under consideration, a motion was made by Mr. [John] Rutledge, seconded by Mr. [John Lewis] Gervais, to strike out the words "and accruing to the use of the United States:"

And on the question, shall those words stand? the yeas and nays being required by by Mr. [John Lewis] Gervais,

State	Member	Vote	State vote
New Hampshire			
	Mr. Gilman,	ay	ay
	White,	ay	
Rhode Island,			
	Mr. Collins,	ay	no
	Arnold,	no	
	Howell,	no	
Connecticut,			
	Mr. Ellsworth,	ay	ay
	Wolcott,	ay	
New York,			
	Mr. Floyd,	no	div.
	Hamilton,	ay	
New Jersey,			
	Mr. Boudinot,	ay	ay
	Clark,	ay	
	Elmer,	ay	
Pennsylvania,			
	Mr. Fitzsimmons,	ay	ay
	Peters,	ay	
	Montgomery,	ay	
Delaware,			
	Mr. McKean,	ay	ay
	Wharton,	ay	
Maryland,			
	Mr. Carroll,	ay	*
Virginia,			
	Mr. Jones,	ay	ay
	Madison,	ay	
North Carolina,			
	Mr. Hawkins,	no	ay
	Williamson,	ay	
	Blount,	ay	
South Carolina,			
	Mr. Rutledge,	no	no
	Ramsay,	no	
	Izard,	no	
	Gervais,	no	

So it was resolved in the affirmative.

The Committee consisting &c. to whom was referred the motion of Mr. [Richard] Peters with respect to keeping the information received by ~~and the parts of the~~ Congress or the proceedings of Con-

[1] This report, in the writing of James Madison, is in the *Papers of the Continental Congress,* No. 19, II, folio 497[b].

FRIDAY, MARCH 28, 1783

Congress resumed the consideration of the report of the committee on the means of restoring and supporting public credit, and of obtaining from the states substantial funds for funding the whole debt of the United States; and the last clause being amended to read as follows:

That as a more convenient and certain rule of ascertaining the proportions to be supplied by the states respectively, to the common treasury, the following alteration in the Articles of Confederation and perpetual union between the states be, and the same is hereby agreed to in Congress, and the several states are advised to authorise their respective delegates to subscribe and ratify the same, as part of the said instrument of union, in the words following, to wit:

Consideration of Article VIII of Confederation and vote, March 28, 1783

"So much of the eighth of the Articles of Confederation and perpetual union, as is contained in the words following, to wit: All charges of war and all other expences that shall be incurred for the common defence or general welfare, and allowed by the United States in Congress assembled, shall be defrayed out of a common treasury, which shall be supplied by the several states in proportion to the value of all land within each State, granted to or surveyed for any person, as such land and the buildings and improvements thereon shall be estimated according to such mode as the United States in Congress assembled shall, from time to time, direct and appoint, is hereby revoked and made void; and in place thereof it is declared and concluded, the same having been agreed to in a Congress of the United States, [that all charges of war and all other expences that have been or shall be incurred for the common defence or general welfare, and allowed by the United States in Congress assembled, except so far as shall be otherwise provided for, shall be defrayed out of a common treasury, which shall be supplied by the several states in proportion to the whole number of free ~~white~~ inhabitants, and ~~one half~~ three-fifths of the number of all other inhabitants of every sex and condition, except Indians not paying taxes in each State; which number shall be triennially taken and transmitted to the United States in Congress assembled, in such mode as they shall direct and appoint"].[1]

A motion was made by Mr. [Theodorick] Bland, seconded by Mr. A[rthur] Lee, that the same be struck out of the report:

And on the question, shall the paragraph, as amended, stand as part of the report? the yeas and nays being required by Mr. [Theodorick] Bland,

New Hampshire,		
Mr. Gilman,	ay	ay
White,	ay	
Massachusetts,		
Mr. Holten,	no	no
Osgood,	no	
Gorham,	ay	
Higginson,	no	
Rhode Island,		
Mr. Collins,	no	no
Arnold,	no	
Connecticut,		
Mr. Wolcott,	no	no
Dyer,	no	
New York,		
Mr. Floyd,	ay	*
New Jersey,		
Mr. Boudinot,	ay	ay
Clark,	ay	
Pennsylvania,		
Mr. Mifflin,	ay	ay
Fitzsimmons,	ay	
Wilson,	ay	
Montgomery,	ay	
Delaware,		
Mr. McComb,	no	no
Bedford,	no	

[1] The part in brackets, in the writing of James Madison, is in the *Papers of the Continental Congress*, No. 26, folio 433. A variation, indorsed upon the report by Madison, is as follows:

in proportion to the number of white Inhabitants of every age sex and condition, and of the ½ of the number of all other inhabitants, which numbers shall be triennially taken and transmitted to the U. S. in Congress assembled in such mode as they shall direct and appoint.

The indorsement states:

"The latter clause of the report of the Comee being recommitted the Committee reported the enclosed in lieu thereof, and motion being made to fill the blank before the words 'the number of all other inhabitants' with the words 'two thirds of' Question taken, 5 ayes 4 noes 2 divided N. H. a. Mass. div. Rh. div. Con. ay. N. J. ay. Pens. ay. Del. ay. Maryland, Virge, N. Co & S. Co no. So the question was lost, and this part relative to an alteration of the art: of Confederation was postponed."

Maryland,			*North Carolina,*		
Mr. T. S. Lee,	ay	ay	Mr. Hawkins,	ay	ay
Hemsley,	ay		Williamson,	ay	
Virginia,			*South Carolina,*		
Mr. Jones,	ay	ay	Mr. Rutledge,	no	no
Madison,	ay		Ramsay,	no	
Bland,	no		Izard,	no	
A. Lee,	no		Gervais,	no	
Mercer,	ay				

So the question was lost, and the paragraph struck out.

SATURDAY, MARCH 29, 1783

A motion was made by Mr. A[rthur] Lee, seconded by Mr. [Samuel] Holten, that the Superintendant of finance do lay before Congress immediately, an account of all monies which were in his hands at his coming into office, or have been received since for the public use, together with the application of all such monies in each month, distinguishing the date of each payment, the person to whom, and the purpose for which such payment was made.

A motion was made by Mr. [Samuel] Osgood, seconded by Mr. [Hugh] Williamson, that the motion be committed:

And on the question for commitment, the yeas and nays being required by Mr. A[rthur] Lee,

New Hampshire,			*New York,*		
Mr. Gilman,	no	no	Mr. Floyd,	ay	ay
White,	no		Hamilton,	ay	
Massachusetts,			*New Jersey,*		
Mr. Holten,	ay	ay	Mr. Boudinot,	ay	div.
Osgood,	ay		Clark,	no	
Gorham,	ay		*Pennsylvania,*		
Higginson,	ay		Mr. Mifflin,	ay	ay
Rhode Island,			Fitzsimmons,	ay	
Mr. Collins,	no	no	Wilson,	ay	
Arnold,	no		Montgomery,	ay	
Connecticut,			*Delaware,*		
Mr. Wolcott,	ay	div.	Mr. McComb,	ay	ay
Dyer,	no		Bedford,	ay	

The paragraph being then amended to read as follows:

That as a more convenient and certain rule of ascertaining the proportions to be supplied by the states respectively to the common treasury, the following alteration in the Articles of Confederation and perpetual union between these states be, and the same is hereby agreed to in Congress, and the several states are advised to authorise their respective delegates to subscribe and ratify the same, as part of the said instrument of union, in the words following, to wit:

So much of the eighth of the Articles of Confederation and perpetual union between the thirteen states of America, as is contained in the words following, to wit:

All charges of war and all other expences that shall be incurred for the common defence or general welfare, and allowed by the United States in Congress assembled, shall be defrayed out of a common treasury, which shall be supplied by the several states in proportion to the value of all land within each state granted to or surveyed for any person, as such land and the buildings and improvements thereon shall be estimated, according to such mode as the United States in Congress assembled shall, from time to time, direct and appoint, is hereby revoked and made void; and in place thereof it is declared and concluded, the same having been agreed to in a Congress of the United States, that "all charges of war and all other expences that have been or shall be incurred for the common defence or general welfare, and allowed by the United States in Congress assembled, except so far as shall be otherwise provided for, shall be defrayed out of a common treasury, which shall be supplied by the several states in proportion to the whole number of white and other free citizens and inhabitants of every age, sex and condition, including those bound to servitude for a term of years, and three-fifths of all other persons not comprehended in the foregoing description, except Indians, not paying taxes, in each state; which

Consideration of Article VIII of Articles of Confederation and vote, April 1, 1783

numbers shall be triennially taken and transmitted to the United States in Congress assembled, in such mode as they shall direct and appoint:

And on the question, shall the clause, as amended, stand part of the report? the yeas and nays being required by Mr. [Theodorick] Bland,

State / Member	Vote	State vote
New Hampshire,		
Mr. White,	ay	*
Massachusetts,		
Mr. Holten,	no	div.
Osgood,	ay	
Gorham,	ay	
Higginson,	no	
Rhode Island,		
Mr. Collins,	no	no
Arnold,	no	
Connecticut,		
Mr. Ellsworth,	ay	ay
Wolcott,	ay	
Dyer,	ay	
New York,		
Mr. Floyd,	ay	ay
Hamilton,	ay	
New Jersey,		
Mr. Boudinot,	ay	ay
Clark,	ay	
Pennsylvania,		
Mr. Fitzsimmons,	ay	ay
Montgomery,	ay	
Peters,	ay	
Delaware,		
Mr. McComb,	ay	*
Maryland,		
Mr. T. S. Lee,	ay	ay
Hemsley,	ay	
Virginia,		
Mr. Jones,	ay	ay
Madison,	ay	
Bland,	no	
Mercer,	ay	
North Carolina,		
Mr. Hawkins,	ay	ay
Williamson,	ay	
South Carolina,		
Mr. Rutledge,	ay	ay
Izard,	ay	

So it was resolved in the affirmative.

On the report of a committee, consisting of Mr. [Abraham] Clark, Mr. [Eliphalet] Dyer, and Mr. [John] Rutledge, to whom was referred the report of the Secretary at War, on a memorial from Colonel Broadhead:

Resolved, That the Superintendant of finance take order for payment to Colonel Broadhead of ninety eight dollars and fifteen ninetieths of a dollar, being the amount of money expended by him in defending several suits brought against him for certain transactions during his command at Fort Pitt:

So it was resolved in the affirmative.][1]

Ordered, That a letter of the 11th of April, from the Superintendant of Finance, proposing the sale of the Ship the *Duc de Lauzun*, be referred to Mr. [Theodorick] Bland, Mr. [Thomas] Fitzsimmons and Mr. [Stephen] Higginson.[2]

TUESDAY, APRIL 15, 1783

Congress took into consideration the articles agreed upon at Paris, on the 30 day of November last, entitled "Articles agreed upon by and between Richard Oswald, esq. the commissioner of his Britannic Majesty, for treating of peace with the commissioners of the United States of America, in behalf of his said Majesty on the one part, and John Adams, Benjamin Franklin, John Jay and Henry Laurens, four of the commissioners of the said states, for treating of peace with the commissioner of his said Majesty, on their behalf, on the other part; to be inserted in, and to constitute the treaty of peace proposed to be concluded between the crown of Great Britain and the said United States; but which treaty is not to be concluded until terms of a peace shall be agreed upon between Great Britain and France, and his Britannic Majesty shall be ready to conclude such treaty accordingly;" and thereupon,

[1] The proclamation and the vote upon it were also entered in the manuscript Secret Journal, Foreign Affairs. The part in brackets was entered in the public Journal by George Bond.

[2] This order was entered only in the journal kept by the Secretary of Congress for the Superintendent of Finance: *Morris Papers, Congressional Proceedings*. The record in Committee Books No. 186 and No. 191 shows that a report was delivered April 18, and acted on, April 21.

On this date, according to the indorsement, a letter of Thomas Chittenden, dated March 18, was read and referred to Mr. [Daniel] Carroll, Mr. [Nathaniel] Gorham, Mr. [Arthur] Lee, Mr. [John Taylor] Gilman, and Mr. [Oliver] Wolcott. It is in the *Papers of the Continental Congress*, No. 40, II, folio 401. See *post*, May 26.

Also a letter of April 11 from the President of the Council of Pennsylvania to the delegates of that State in Congress asking that measures be taken to secure negroes belonging to citizens of that State. It is in No. 69, II, folio 439.

Reading in Congress of a letter from the President of the Council of Pennsylvania, April 15, 1783

On April 14, according to the indorsement, was read a letter of April 9, from General Washington. It is in No. 152, XI, folio 211.

Resolved, That ~~the Secretary for foreign affairs be directed~~ a committee ~~of Congress~~ be appointed to prepare and lay before Congress ~~without delay~~ a draft of a ratification of the ~~provisional treaty~~ articles entered into between the Commissioners of the United States and the Commissioner of his Britannic Majesty at Paris on the 30th day of November last.

Resolved, That the Commander in Chief be directed to enter into ~~the necessary~~ preparatory arrangements relative to the 7th Article of the said Treaty with the Commanders in Chief of the British land and naval forces in America, and that a committee be appointed to prepare a letter to him on this subject.[1]

Resolved, unanimously, That the said articles be ratified, and that a ratification in due form be sent to our Ministers Plenipotentiary at the Court of Versailles, to be exchanged if an exchange shall be necessary.

Resolved, That the agent of marine cause all the naval prisoners to be set at liberty.

Resolution,
April 15, 1783

Resolved, That the Commander in Chief be, and he is hereby instructed to make the proper arrangements with the Commander in Chief of the British forces, for receiving possession of the posts in the United States occupied by the troops of his Britannic Majesty; and for obtaining the delivery of all negroes and other property of the inhabitants of

[1] This report, in the writing of Alexander Hamilton, is in the *Papers of the Continental Congress*, No. 25, II, folio 197. The indorsement states that it was agreed to on this day.

To this period belongs the following motion, in the writing of James Wilson, except the words in brackets, which are added in pencil by Alexander Hamilton. It is on folio 196, and is undated:

"And whereas it was agreed between the Ministers Plenipotentiary of the United States and the Minister Plenipotentiary of his Britannic Majesty, that all hostilities should cease between the said United States their subjects and possessions, and his Britannic Majesty his subjects and possessions at the terms and epochs agreed upon between their most Christian [Catholic] and Britannic Majesties.

And whereas the ratification of the said preliminary articles between their most Christian and Britannic Majesties were exchanged by their Ministers on the third day of Feby. last, [and between the Ministers of their Britannic and Catholic Majesties on the 9th of said month].

And whereas it is our will and pleasure that the cessation of hostilities between the United States of America and his Britannic Majesty should be agreeable to the said terms and epochs [fixed between their Christian and Britannic Majesties].

We have &c."

the United States in the possession of the British forces, or any subjects of, or adherents to his said Britannic Majesty; and that the Secretary at War, in conjunction with the Commander in Chief, take proper arrangements for setting at liberty all land prisoners.

When the foregoing resolution was under debate, a motion was made by Mr. [Abraham] Clark, seconded by Mr. [Eliphalet] Dyer, to strike out the words "in conjunction with the Commander in Chief":

And on the question, shall those words stand? the yeas and nays being required by Mr. [Hugh] Williamson,

State / Member	Vote	State vote
New Hampshire,		
Mr. White,	no	*
Massachusetts,		
Mr. Holten,	ay	ay
Gorham,	ay	
Rhode Island,		
Mr. Arnold,	ay	*
Connecticut,		
Mr. Ellsworth,	no	no
Dyer,	no	
New York,		
Mr. Floyd,	ay	ay
Hamilton,	ay	
New Jersey,		
Mr. Boudinot,	ay	div.
Clark,	no	
Pennsylvania,		
Mr. Fitzsimmons,	ay	ay
Peters,	ay	
Delaware,		
Mr. Bedford,	ay	*
Maryland,		
Mr. T. S. Lee,	ay	ay
Carroll,	ay	
Virginia,		
Mr. Jones,	ay	ay
Madison,	ay	
Bland,	ay	
North Carolina,		
Mr. Hawkins,	ay	ay
Williamson,	ay	
South Carolina,		
Mr. Rutledge,	ay	ay
Izard,	ay	
Gervais,	ay	

So it was resolved in the affirmative.

Resolved, That the form of the ratification be as follows:

The United States in Congress assembled, To all who shall see these presents Greeting:

Whereas in and by our commission dated at Philadelphia the fifteenth day of June in the year of our Lord one thousand seven hundred and eighty one the hon^ble John Adams,

persons may have paid on purchasing any of the said lands, rights or properties since the confiscation.

And it is agreed, that all persons who have any interest in confiscated lands, either by debts, marriage settlements or otherwise, shall meet with no lawful impediment in the prosecution of their just rights.

ARTICLE VI

That there shall be no future confiscations made, nor prosecutions commenced against any person or persons for or by reason of the part which he or they may have taken in the present war; and that no person shall, on that account, suffer any future loss or damage either in his person, liberty or property, and that those who may be in confinement on such charges, at the time of the ratification of the treaty in America, shall be immediately set at liberty, and the prosecutions so commenced be discontinued.

ARTICLE VII

There shall be a firm and perpetual peace between his Britannick Majesty and the said states, and between the subjects of the one and the citizens of the other; wherefore all hostilities both by sea and land shall then immediately cease: all prisoners on both sides shall be set at liberty, and his Britannick Majesty shall, with all convenient speed, and without causing any destruction, or carrying away any negroes or other property of the American inhabitants, withdraw all his armies, garrisons and fleets from the said United States, and from every port, place and harbour within the same; leaving in all fortifications the American artillery that may be therein; and shall also order and cause all archives, records, deeds and papers belonging to any of said states, or their citizens, which in the course of the war may have fallen into the hands of his

Treaty of Peace, as ratified April 15, 1782

officers, to be forthwith restored and delivered to the proper states and persons to whom they belong.

ARTICLE VIII

The navigation of the river Mississippi, from its source to the ocean, shall forever remain free and open to the subjects of Great Britain, and the citizens of the United States.

ARTICLE IX

In case it should so happen, that any place or territory belonging to Great Britain or to the United States should be conquered by the arms of either from the other, before the arrival of these articles in America, it is agreed, that the same shall be restored without difficulty, and without requiring any compensation.

Done at Paris, the thirtieth day of November, one thousand seven hundred and eighty-two.

(Signed) RICHARD OSWALD, [L. S.]
JOHN ADAMS, [L. S.]
B. FRANKLIN, [L. S.]
JOHN JAY, [L. S.]
HENRY LAURENS, [L. S.]

Witnesses.

(Signed) CALEB WHITEFORD,
Secretary to the British Commission.
W. T. FRANKLIN,
Secretary to the American Commission.

SEPARATE ARTICLE

It is hereby understood and agreed, that in case Great Britain, at the conclusion of the present war, shall recover, or be put in possession of West Florida, the line of north boundary between the said province and the United States shall be a line drawn from the

of Confederation and perpetual union, between these states be, and the same is hereby agreed to in Congress; and the several states are advised to authorise their respective delegates to subscribe and ratify the same as part of the said instrument of union, in the words following, to wit:

So much of the 8th of the Articles of Confederation and perpetual union, between the thirteen states of America, as is contained in the words following, to wit:

"All charges of war and all other expences that shall be incurred for the common defence or general welfare, and allowed by the United States in Congress assembled, shall be defrayed out of a common treasury, which shall be supplied by the several states in proportion to the value of all land within each State granted to or surveyed for any person, as such land and the buildings and improvements thereon shall be estimated according to such mode as the United States in Congress assembled shall, from time to time, direct and appoint," is hereby revoked and made void; and in place thereof it is declared and concluded, the same having been agreed to in a Congress of the United States, that "all charges of war and all other expences that have been or shall be incurred for the common defence or general welfare, and allowed by the United States in Congress assembled, except so far as shall be otherwise provided for, shall be defrayed out of a common treasury, which shall be supplied by the several states in proportion to the whole number of white and other free citizens and inhabitants, of every age, sex and condition, including those bound to servitude for a term of years, and three-fifths of all other persons not comprehended in the foregoing description, except Indians, not paying taxes, in each State; which number shall be triennially taken and transmitted to the United States in Congress assembled, in such mode as they shall direct and appoint."[1]

Consideration of Article VIII of Confederation and vote, April 18, 1782

[1] This report is in the *Papers of the Continental Congress*, No. 26, folio 415. A printed copy of the report of March 18 was used, and altered by Charles Thomson, to satisfy the changes made by Congress. A printed copy of the resolutions, with those of February 17, is in No. 56, folio 447.

On the question to agree to the foregoing act, the yeas and nays being required by Mr. [Jonathan] Arnold,

New Hampshire,			*Delaware,*		
Mr. White,	ay	*	Mr. McComb,	ay	ay
Massachusetts,			Bedford,	ay	
Mr. Holton,	ay	ay	*Maryland,*		
Osgood,	ay		Mr. T. S. Lee,	ay	ay
Gorham,	ay		Carroll,	ay	
Higginson,	no		*Virginia,*		
Rhode Island,			Mr. Jones,	ay	ay
Mr. Collins,	no	no	Madison,	ay	
Arnold,	no		Bland,	ay	
Connecticut,			Mercer,	ay	
Mr. Ellsworth,	ay	ay	*North Carolina,*		
Dyer,	ay		Mr. Hawkins,	ay	ay
New York,			Williamson,	ay	
Mr. Floyd,	ay	div.	*South Carolina,*		
Hamilton,	no		Mr. Rutledge,	ay	ay
New Jersey,			Izard,	ay	
Mr. Boudinot,	ay	ay	Gervais,	ay	
Clark,	ay				
Condict,	ay				
Pennsylvania,					
Mr. Fitzsimmons,	ay	ay			
Peters,	ay				

So it was resolved in the affirmative.[1]

That the money to arise from the said duty be appropriated and applied to payment of the annual interest at 6 per cent. of the debt due to the army of the U. S. and the surplus from time to time, towards sinking the principal or to payment of the interest and principal of the money which may be borrowed for discharging the said debt to the army, and to no other purpose whatsoever. And that the said duty be continued, until the debts above mentioned shall be fully paid and satisfied.

Negatived.[2]

That the resolutions of the instant be transmitted to the several states ~~by their Delegates~~ with a circular letter from the President to the Executive of each State, requesting that the said resolu-

[1] Here Charles Thomson resumes the entries in the Journal.

[2] This motion, undated, in the writing of John Rutledge, is in the *Papers of the Continental Congress*, No. 36, II, folio 21.

The committee [Mr. Theodorick Bland, Mr. Alexander Hamilton, and Mr. Eliphalet Dyer] to whom was referred the memorial of Rev J. P. Tetard, are fully satisfied that his services, sufferings and sacrifices in the cause of America have been as set forth in the said memorial, but in their opinion the prayer of the memorial cannot with propriety be granted.[1]

[1] This report, in the writing of Theodorick Bland, is in the *Papers of the Continental Congress*, No. 42, VII, folio 445. Committee Book, No. 186, gives it this date but the indorsement gives it May 17. John Peter Tetard's memorial, dated Philadelphia, 8th May, 1783, was read and referred to committee May 12, and is on folio 443.

On this day, as the indorsement states, a memorial of the officers of the Navy, praying for relief, dated Philadelphia, April 28, 1783, was referred to Mr. [John] Collins, Mr. [Abraham] Clark and Mr. [William] Hemsley. The indorsement further says it was "Answered by Act August 1st, 1787." It is in No. 41, VII, folio 99. According to Committee Books No. 186 and No. 191 the committee was renewed August 5, and the memorial referred on that date to Mr. [Abraham] Clark, Mr. [John Francis] Mercer and Mr. [William] Ellery, who delivered a report August 19.

Also a memorial of James McKenzie and others, sailors on the *Bon Homme Richard*, praying for relief. It was dated May 14, and on May 16 was referred to the Agent of Marine to report. It is in No. 137, II, folio 601. See *post*, September 15.

On May 19, according to the indorsement, was read a letter of May 14 from General Washington. It is in No. 152, XI, folio 275.

Receipt of letter, May 16, 1783

Also, on May 19, according to the indorsement, Mr. [Theodorick] Bland laid before Congress a communication, of the same date, from James Belsches, Jr., relative to the difficulty of recovering negroes from the British. It is in No. 78, IV, folio 395.

Also, on May 19, a letter, of the same date, from the Secretary at War, transmitting a letter from General Washington, with a copy of one from Dr. James Craik, was referred to Mr. [Eliphalet] Dyer, Mr. [Hugh] Williamson and Mr. [Richard] Peters. The Secretary's letter is in No. 149, II, folio 585; Washington's letter is on folio 581, and a copy of Dr. Craik's letter on folio 577. According to Committee Books 186 and 191, a report was rendered June 10, 1783, and negatived April 16, 1784.

The following report, in the writing of Eliphalet Dyer, is marked "Col. Dyer's essay," and is on folio 575:

~~Your committee having taken into consideration the representation of Craige and General Washington's letter thereon are of opinion that as the commutation proposed to Congress and by them adopted was founded wholly on their previous engagements for half pay and that notwithstanding the merits of any particular gentleman in either of the Departments to which the half pay could be applied, it would be attended with very great inconvenience to enter into a comparative view of the particular circumstances of every person concerned as in that case if it should appear that any of the officers in a comparative view of the time of their services or other circumstances should not be equally entitled with others yet Congress could not diminish from the substance of their contract, so on the other hand, it will not be proper to make any addition but the whole being considered in a collective view no addition or diminution can with propriety be made therein.~~

Maryland,			*North Carolina,*		
Mr. Carroll,	no	no	Mr. Hawkins,	no	no
Hemsley,	no		Williamson,	no	
Virginia,			*South Carolina,*		
Mr. Madison,	no		Mr. Rutledge,	no	
Bland,	no	no	Izard,	no	no
Mercer,	no		Gervais,	no	

So the question was lost.

Motion, May 23, 1783

[Motion of John Francis Mercer, seconded by Ralph Izard.]

Whereas Sir Guy Carleton has not given such reasons for continuing with the British forces in the garrison of New York as are satisfactory to Congress: and whereas the said Sir Guy Carleton has suffered many negroes the property of the citizens of these United States to be carried off, contrary to the 7th article of the Preliminary Treaty,

Resolved, That it is not expedient at present to disband or furlough the army of the United States.—Withdrawn.[1]

The Agent of Marine to whom was referred the Memorial of Seth Harding, begs leave to report,

That the Memorialist appears to be among the number of public creditors whose Claims must come before the Commissioner to be appointed for the purposes of liquidating and finally settling the accounts of the Marine Department up to the last day of December 1781; that he expects a proper person will soon be named for that business and then the accounts of the memorialist will come in course for settlement. For the ballance that shall appear to be due, he will partake of such relief as the public funds may then be in a situation to afford, but that at present the prayer of his memorial can not be complied with.

All which is humbly submitted

ROBT. MORRIS

MARINE OFFICE *22 May 1783.*[2]

The committee of the week [Mr. Thomas FitzSimons, Mr. Ralph Izard, and Mr. Eliphalet Dyer] report, upon the petition of Eleazer Levy respecting a mortgage which he holds upon the lands at West Point,

[1] This motion, in the writing of Ralph Izard, is in the *Papers of the Continental Congress,* No. 36, II, folio 127. The indorsement gives it this date.

[2] This report is in the *Papers of the Continental Congress,* No. 137, II, folio 489. It was read on this day, according to the indorsement.

The Committee to whom was refered the Letter of the 15 inst from the Superintendant of Finance respecting the appointment of an Agent at Havana, beg leave to report,

That in their opinion it is highly necessary an agent should immediately be appointed for that service.[1]

Resolved, That another agent be appointed for that service.

Ordered, That to-morrow be assigned for the election.

On motion of Mr. [Alexander] Hamilton, seconded by Mr. [Ralph] Izard,

Whereas by the articles agreed upon on the 30 of November last by and between ~~Richard Oswald Esqr. the commissioner of his Britannic Majesty for treating of peace with the commissioners of the United States of America in behalf of his said Majesty on the one part, and John Adams, Benjamin Franklin, John Jay and Henry Laurens, four of the commissioners of the said States for treating of peace with the commissioner of his said Majesty on their behalf, on the other part, to be inserted in and to constitute the treaty of peace proposed to be concluded between the Crown of Great Britain and the said United States,~~ the commissioners of the United States of America for making peace, and the commissioner on the part of his Britannic Majesty, it is stipulated,

Resolution,
May 26, 1783

That his Britannic Majesty shall, with all convenient speed, and without causing any destruction, or carrying away any negroes or other property of the American inhabitants, withdraw all his armies, garrisons and fleets from the said United States, and from every port, place and harbour within the same: and whereas a considerable number of negroes belonging to the citizens of these states, have been carried off therefrom, contrary to the true intent and meaning of the said articles:

Resolved, That copies of the letters between the Commander in Chief and Sir Guy Carleton, and other papers on this sub-

[1] This report, in the writing of Thomas FitzSimons, is in the *Papers of the Continental Congress,* No. 19, IV, folio 397. The letter of the Superintendent of Finance is on folio 401.

ject, be transmitted to the ministers plenipotentiary of these states for negotiating a peace in Europe; and that they be directed to remonstrate thereon to the Court of Great Britain, and ~~use their utmost endeavors to obtain~~ take proper measures for obtaining such reparation as the nature of the case will admit.

Ordered, That a copy of the foregoing resolve be transmitted to the Commander in Chief; and that he be directed to continue his remonstrances to Sir Guy Carleton, respecting the permitting negroes belonging to the citizens of these states to leave New York, and to ~~endeavor to prevail with him to discontinue~~ insist on the discontinuance of that measure.[1]

On motion of Mr. [Alexander] Hamilton, seconded by Mr. [Stephen] Higginson,

Resolved, That the Commander in Chief be instructed to grant furloughs to the non-commissioned officers and soldiers in the service of the United States, inlisted to serve during the war, who shall be discharged as soon as the definitive treaty of peace is concluded, together with a proportionable number of commissioned officers of the different grades; and that the Secretary at War and Commander in Chief take the proper measures for conducting those troops to their respective ~~states~~ homes, in such a manner as may be most convenient to themselves, and to the states through which they may pass; and that the men thus furloughed be allowed to take their arms with them ~~the resolution of to the contrary notwithstanding.~~[2]

On motion of Mr. [Hugh] Williamson, seconded by Mr. [Benjamin] Hawkins,

Resolved, That the commanding officer in the southern department be also instructed to grant furloughs to the

[1] This motion, in the writing of John Rutledge, is in the *Papers of the Continental Congress*, No. 36, II, folio 129. It was also entered in the manuscript Secret Journal, Foreign Affairs.

[2] This motion, in the writing of Hugh Williamson, is in the *Papers of the Continental Congress*, No. 36, II, folio 131. A note on the motion says: "made by Col. Hamilton, 2d by Mr. Williamson."

MONDAY, SEPTEMBER 1, 1783

An act of the general assembly of Connecticut, authorising the delegates of that State, to agree to an alteration in the 8th of the Articles of Confederation as recommended by the act of the 18 of April last, was laid before Congress and read, as follows:

(L. S.) At a general Assembly of the Governor and Company of the State of Connecticut, holden at Hartford in the said State, on the second Thursday of May, Anno Domini, 1783.

Whereas the United States in Congress assembled, on the 18th day of April, 1783, among other things resolved, that a more convenient and certain rule of ascertaining the proportions to be supplied by the states respectively, to the common treasury, the following alteration in the Articles of Confederation and perpetual union between these states be, and the same is hereby agreed to in Congress: and the several states are advised to authorise their respective delegates to subscribe and ratify the same, as a part of the said instrument of union, in the words following, viz. So much of the 8th of the Articles of Confederation and perpetual union between the thirteen States of America, as is contained in the words following, to wit: "All charges of war, and all other expences that shall be incurred for the common defence or general welfare, and allowed by the United States in Congress assembled, shall be defrayed out of a common treasury, which shall be supplied by the several states, in proportion to the value of all lands within each State, granted to or surveyed for any person, as such land, and the buildings and improvements thereon, shall be estimated according to such mode as the United States in Congress assembled shall, from time to time, direct and appoint," is hereby revoked and made void, and in place thereof it is declared and concluded, the same having been agreed to in a Congress of the United States, "that all charges of war, and other expences that have been or shall be incurred for the common defence or general welfare, and allowed by the United States in Congress assembled, except so far as shall be otherwise provided for, shall be defrayed out of a common treasury, which shall be supplied by the

Resolution of Connecticut general assembly concerning Eighth Article of Confederation, as read September 1, 1783

several states in proportion to the whole number of white and other free citizens and inhabitants of every age, sex and condition, including those bound to servitude for a term of years, and three fifths of all other persons not comprehended in the foregoing description, except Indians not paying taxes in each State, which number shall be triennially taken and transmitted to the United States in Congress assembled, in such mode as they shall direct and appoint."

It is resolved, and enacted by this assembly, that the delegates of this State, in the Congress of the United States, or any two or more of them, be, and they are hereby fully authorised and empowered, on behalf of this State, to subscribe and ratify the afore-recited alteration in the 8th of the Articles of Confederation and perpetual union between the United States of America, as a part of the said instrument of union.[1]

The delegates for the State of Pensylvania, laid before Congress sundry resolutions of the general assembly of that State, which were read and ordered to be entered on the Journal as follows:

"State of Pensylvania, in General Assembly, Friday, August 29, 1783, A. M.

The report of the committee appointed to consider of the most eligible means for the accommodation of Congress, should that honorable body determine to reside within this State, read August 27 instant, was read the second time; whereupon,

Resolved unanimously, That until Congress shall determine upon the place of their permanent residence, it would be highly agreeable to this house, if that honorable body should deem it expedient to return to and continue in the city of Philadelphia; in which case they offer to Congress the different apartments in the state-house and adjacent buildings which they formerly occupied for the purpose of transacting the national business therein.

Resolved unanimously, That this house will take effectual measures to enable the executive of the State to afford speedy and adequate support and protection to the honor and dignity of the United States in Congress, and the persons of those composing the supreme council of the nation assembled in this city.

[1] This act is in the *Papers of the Continental Congress,* No. 75, folio 77.

enjoy all the rights, liberties, privileges, immunities and exemptions in trade, navigation and commerce whether in passing from one port in the said States to another, or in going to or from the same, from and to any part of the world which the said subjects enjoy. And the said Citizens of the U. S. shall conform themselves to the Laws and Ordinances which are or shall be made relative to trade and commerce with the Kingdom of Denmark and the Territories thereunto belonging, not contravening this Treaty, in like manner as the said subjects are bound to observe them.[1]

THURSDAY, OCTOBER 23, 1783

The order of the day being called for, to take into consideration the report of a committee on a military peace arrangement,

The Committee consisting of M^r [Alexander] Hamilton, M^r [James] Madison, M^r [Oliver] Ellsworth, M^r [James] Wilson and M^r [Samuel] Holten, "appointed to take into consideration the arrangements proper to be taken in case of a general peace" observe with respect to a Military peace establishment that before any plan can with propriety be adopted it is necessary to enquire what powers exist for that purpose in the Confederation.

By the 4th clause of the 6th Article, it is declared that "no vessels of war shall be kept up by any State in time of peace except such number only as shall be deemed necessary by the United States in Congress Assembled for the defence of such State or its trade, nor shall any body of forces be kept up by any State in time of peace, except such number only as in the judgment of the United States in Congress Assembled shall be deemed requisite to garrison the forts necessary for the defence of such State."

Committee report on Ninth Article of Confederation, as read October 23, 1783

By the 5th clause of the 9th Article the United States in Congress Assembled are empowered generally and without mention of peace or war "to build and equip a navy, to agree upon the number of land forces and to make requisitions from each State for its quota in proportion to the number of white inhabitants in each State, which requisition shall be binding and thereupon the legislature of each

[1] This report, in the writing of Arthur Lee, is in the *Papers of the Continental Congress*, No. 25, II, folio 315. The indorsement states that it was delivered on this day, entered and read. According to the record in Committee Book No. 191, it was taken up in December by the committee on the letters from Ministers at Paris.

Also, was read a letter of August 25 from Governor Lyman Hall of Georgia relative to payment of debts and representation. It is in No. 73, folio 307.

and commerce, and to negotiate and sign the same, transmitting them to Congress for their final ratification, and that such Commission be in force for a term not exceeding two years.

~~That the said ministers be instructed to notify to the powers with whom they may negotiate the great value at which these states will esteem their friendship and connection and that it will be their constant endeavour to promote a good understanding and harmony with them and to prevent everything which might interrupt it by every means in their power, but that the heavy debt which they have contracted during the late war and the state of desolation and depopulation in which every part of these states were left by it have rendered it inconvenient at present for them to keep ministers resident at the courts of Europe, and they hope that this deviation from the practice of friendly nations may be ascribed to its true cause and not to any want of respect to their friends or of attachment to treaties, to the faithful observance of which they shall at all times pay the most earnest attention.~~

That consuls be appointed for the ports of and consuls general be established at

~~[That the said Ministers be instructed in their negociations with the foreign Court to urge with perseverance the necessity of a reasonable forbearance in the levy of debts due within these states to British subjects, the establishment of the idea of these states that all demands for interest accruing during the war would be highly inequitable and unjust; and the expediency of settling this by precise stipulation in order to avoid those mutual complaints and altercations which may disturb the harmony of the two nations.~~

(That the said Ministers to be Commissioned for treating with foreign nations be referred to the instructions of the thirtieth day of May 1783, relative to British debts, the objects of which they are hereby directed to urge with perseverance.)

That they require with firmness and decision full satisfaction for all slaves and other property belonging to citizens of these States taken and carried away in violation of the preliminary and definitive articles of peace; and to enable them to do this on precise grounds Congress will furnish them with necessary facts and documents.][1]

Committee report recommending instructions to ministers in Europe for peace treaty negotiations, as read December 22, 1783

That Doctor Franklin be desired to notify to the Apostolical Nuncio at Versailles, that Congress will always be pleased to testify their respect to his Sovereign and State, but that the subject of his

[1] The words in brackets are in the writing of Thomas Jefferson, except the paragraph in parentheses, which is in the writing of Jacob Read.

James Madison's Notes of Debates, concerning committee report on land valuation for taxation, January 15, 1783

The Committee were in general strongly impressed with the extreme difficulty & inequality if not impracticability of fulfilling the article of Confederation relative to this point; Mr. Rutledge however excepted, who altho' he did not think the rule so good a one as a census of inhabitants, thought it less impracticable than the other members. And if the valuation of lands had not been prescribed by ye federal articles, the Committee w^d certainly have preferred some other rule of apportionment, particularly that of numbers under certain qualifications as to Slaves. As the federal Constitution however left no option, & a few [1] only were disposed to recommend to the States an alteration of it, it was necessary to proceed 1st to settle its meaning—2dly to settle the least objectionable mode of valuation. On the first point, it was doubted by several members whe^r the returns which the report under consideration required from the States would not be final and whether the Art^s of Conf^n w^d allow Congress to alter them after they had fixed on this mode; on this point no vote was taken. A 2^d question afterwards raised in the course of the discussion was how far the Art. required a specific valuation, and how far it gave a latitude as to the mode; on this point also there was a diversity of opinions, but no vote taken.

2dly As to the mode itself referred to the G^d Com^e, it was strongly objected to by the Delegate from Con^t, Mr. Dyer—by Mr. Hamilton,—by Mr. Wilson, by Mr. Carol, and by Mr. Madison, as leaving the States too much to the bias of interest, as well as too uncertain & tedious in the execution. In fav^r of the Rep^t was Mr. Rutledge the father of it, who thought the honor of the States & their mutual confidence a sufficient security ag^st frauds and the suspicion of them. Mr. Ghoram fav^d the report also, as the least impracticable mode, and as it was necessary to attempt at least some compliance with the federal rule before any attempt could be properly made to vary it. An opinion entertained by Massachusetts that she was comparatively in advance to the U. S. made her anxious for a speedy settlement of the mode by which a final apportionment of the common burden c^d be effected. The sentiments of the other members of the Committee were not expressed.

Mr. Hamilton proposed in lieu of a reference of the valuation to the States, to class the lands throughout the States under distinctive descriptions, viz: arable, pasture, wood, &c. and to annex a uniform

[1] Mr. Hamilton was most strenuous on this point. Mr. Wilson also fav^d the idea. Mr. Madison also but restrained in some measure by the declared sense of Vir^a. Mr. Ghoram, and several others also, but wishing previous experience. [Note in MS.]

ing out the idea of separate appropriations of her revenue unless provision were made for the public creditors, by the deplorable & dishonorable situation of public affairs which had compelled Congress to draw bills on the unpromised and contingent bounty of their Ally, and which was likely to banish the Superint. of Finance, whose place cd. not be Supplied, from his department. He observed that he had not introduced detail[s] into the debate because he thought them premature, until a general principle should be fixed; and that as soon as the principle sd. be fixed he would, altho not furnished with any digested plan, contribute all in his power to the forming such a one.

Mr. Rutledge moved that the proposition might be committed in order that some practicable plan might be reported, before Congress sd. declare that it ought to be adopted.

Mr. Izard 2ded. the motion, from a conciliating view.

Mr. Madison thought the commitment unnecessary, and would have the appearance of delay; that too much delay had already taken place, that the deputation of the army had a right to expect an answer to their memorial as soon as it could be decided by Congress. He differed from Mr. Wilson in thinking that a specification of the objects of a general revenue would be improper, and thought that those who doubted of its practicabily. had a right to expect proof of it from details before they cd. be expected to assent to the general principle; but he differed also from Mr. Rutledge, who thought a commitment necessary for the purpose; since his views would be answered by leaving the motion before the house and giving the debate a greater latitude. He suggested as practicable objects of a general revenue. 1st. an impost on trade; 2dly. a poll tax under certain qualifications; 3dly. a land-tax under do.[1]

Mr. Hamilton suggested a house & window tax; he was in favor of the mode of conducting the discussion urged by Mr. Madison.

On the motion for the commt., 6 States were in favor of it, & five agst. it, so it was lost, in this vote the merits of the main proposition very little entered.

Mr. Lee said that it was a waste of time to be forming resolutions & settling principles on this subject. He asked whether these wd. ever bring any money into the public treasury. His opinion was that

[1] A poll tax to be qualified by rating blacks somewhat lower than whites—a land tax by considering the value of land in each State to be in an inverse proportion of its quantity to the no. of people; and apportioning on the aggregate quantity in each State accordingly, leaving the State at liberty to make a distributive apportionment on its several districts, on a like or any other equalizing principle. [Note in MS.]

James Madison's Notes of Debates, concerning debate on taxation, January 28, 1783

and complete adjustment of all accounts between the U. S. and individual States, all reasonable expences which shall have been incurred by the States without the sanction of Cong^{s}, in their defence agst or attacks upon British or Savage enemies, either by sea or by land, and which shall be supported by satisfactory proofs, shall be considered as part of the common charges incident to the present war, and be allowed as such:

(11.) That as a more convenient and certain rule of ascertaining the proportions to be supplied by the States respectively to the common Treasury, the following alteration in the articles of confederation and perpetual union between these States, be and the same is hereby, agreed to in Congress, & the several States are advised to authorize their respective delegates to subscribe and ratify the same, as part of the said instrument of Union, in the words following, to wit.

James Madison's Notes of Debates, concerning committee report on revenue, March 7, 1783

(12.) "So much of the 8th of the Articles of Confederation & perpetual Union between the thirteen States of America as is contained in the words following to wit 'All charges of war &c (to the end of the paragraph)'—is hereby revoked and made void, and in place thereof, it is declared and Concluded, the same having been agreed to in a Congress of the United States, that all charges of war, and all other expences that shall be incurred for the common defence or general welfare and allowed by the U. S. in Congress assembled shall be defrayed out of a common treasury, which shall be supplied by the several States in proportion to the number of inhabitants of every age, sex & condition, except Indians not paying taxes in each State; which number shall be triennially taken & transmitted to the U. S. in Cong^{s} assembled, in such mode as they shall direct and appoint; provided always that in such numeration no persons shall be included who are bound to servitude for life, according to the laws of the State to which they belong, other than such as may be between the ages of [1] ———."

[1] In the draught as laid before the Com^{e} by ——— the (7) paragraph was placed last of all, so as to render the plan indivisible. In the (10) paragraph the word "reasonable" before the word "expences," was not inserted; but to the paragraph was added "provided that this allowance shall not be extended to any expences which shall be declared by nine votes in Congress to be manifestly unreasonable." In other respects the original draught was unaltered, except that a former resolution of Congress in the words of the (6) paragraph was incorporated by the Sec^{y} before it went to the press. [Note in MS.]

brought with them the Spirit of advocates for their respective States rather than of impartial judges between them. He moved that the clause with Mr. Wilson's proposition be recommitted; which was agreed to without opposition.

(11 and 12 Parag[hs]). Mr. Bland opposed it: s[d] that the value of land was the best rule, and that at any rate no change s[d] be attempted untill its practicability s[d] be tried.

Mr. Madison thought the value of land, could never be justly or satisfactorily obtained; that it w[d] ever be a source of contentions among the States, and that as a repetition of the valuation would be within the course of the 25 years, it w[d] unless exchanged for a more simple rule mar the whole plan.

Mr. Ghorum was in fav[r] of the parag[hs]. He represented in strong terms the inequality & clamors produced by valuations of land in the State of Mass[ts] & the probability of the evils being increased among the States themselves which were less tied together & more likely to be jealous of each other.

Mr. Williamson was in fav[r] of the parag[hs].

Mr. Wilson was strenuous in favor of it, s[d] he was in Cong[s] when the Article of Confederation directing a value of land was agreed to, that it was the effect of the impossibility of compromising the different ideas of the Eastern and Southern States as to the value of Slaves compared with the Whites, the alternative in question.

James Madison's Notes of Debates, concerning debate on land and slaves valuation for taxation, March 27 and March 28, 1783

Mr. Clarke was in favor of it. He said that he was also in Cong[s] when this article was decided; that the Southern States w[d] have agreed to numbers, in preference to the value of land if ½ their Slaves only s[d] be included; but that the Eastern States would not concur in that proportion.

It was agreed on all sides that, instead of fixing the proportion by ages, as the report proposed, it would be best to fix the proportion in absolute numbers. With this view & that the blank might be filled up, the clause was recommitted.

FRIDAY MARCH 28.

The Com[e] last ment[d] reported that two blacks be rated as equal to one freeman.

Mr. Wolcott was for rating them as 4 to 3.

Mr. Carrol as 4 to 1.

Mr. Williamson s[d] he was principled ag[st] slavery; and that he thought slaves an incumbrance to Society instead of increasing its ability to pay taxes.

Mr. Higginson as 4 to 3.

Mr. Rutledge s^{d}, for the sake of the object he w^{d} agree to rate Slaves as 2 to 1, but he sincerely thought 3 to 1 would be a juster proportion.

Mr. Holten as 4 to 3.

Mr. Osgood s^{d} he c^{d} not go beyond 4 to 3.

On a question for rating them as 3 to 2 the votes were N. H., ay. Mas., no. R. I., div^{d}. Con^{t}, ay. N. J., ay. P^{a}, ay. Del^{r}, ay. Mary^{d}, no. Virg^{a}, no. N. C., no. S. C., no.

The Paragraph was then postponed by general consent, some wishing for further time to deliberate on it; but it appearing to be the general opinion that no compromise w^{d} be agreed to.

After some further discussions on the report in which the necessity of some simple and practicable rule of apportionment came fully into view, Mr. Madison said that in order to give a proof of the sincerity of his professions of liberality, he w^{d} propose that Slaves should be rated as 5 to 3. Mr. Rutledge 2^{ded} the motion. Mr. Wilson s^{d} he would sacrifice his opinion to this compromise.

Mr. Lee was agst changing the rule, but gave it as his opinion that 2 slaves were not equal to 1 freeman.

On the question for 5 to 3 it passed in the affirmative N. H. ay. Mass. div^{d} R. I., no. Con^{t} no. N. J. ay. P^{a}, ay Mary^{d}, ay. V^{a}, ay. N. C. ay. S. C. ay.

A motion was then made by Mr. Bland, 2^{ded} by Mr. Lee to strike out the clause so amended and on the question "shall it stand" it passed in the negative; N. H. ay. Mas: no. R. I. no. Conn. no. N. J., ay. P^{a}, ay. Del. no. Mar. ay. Virg^{a}, ay. N. C., ay. S. C., no; so the clause was struck out.

The arguments used by those who were for rating slaves high were, that the expence of feeding & cloathing them was as far below that incident to freemen as their industry & ingenuity were below those of freemen; and that the warm climate within wch the States having slaves lay, compared wth the rigorous climate & inferior fertility of the others, ought to have great weight in the case & that the exports of the former States were greater than of the latter. On the other side it was said that Slaves were not put to labour as young as the children of laboring families—that, having no interest in their labor, they did as little as possible, & omitted every exertion of thought requisite to facilitate & expedite it; that if the exports of the States having slaves exceeded those of the others, their imports were in proportion, slaves being employed wholly in agriculture, not in manufactures; & that in fact the balance of trade formerly was much more agst the S^{o} States than the others.

On the main question see Journals.

Mr. Mercer expressed great disquietude at this information, considered it as a dangerous precedent, & that it behoved the Gentleman to explain fully the objects of the Convention, as it would be necessary for the S. States to be otherwise very circumspect in agreeing to any plans on a supposition that the general confederacy was to continue.

Mr. Osgood said that the sole object was to guard ag^st^ an interference of taxes among the States, whose local situation required such precautions; and that if nothing was definitively concluded without the previous communication to & sanction of Cong^s^, the Confederation could not be said to be in any manner departed from; but that in fact nothing was intended that could be drawn within the purview of the federal articles.

Mr. Bland said he had always considered those Conventions as improper & contravening the spirit of the federal Governm^t^ He said they had the appearance of young Congresses.

Mr. Ghorum explains as Mr. Osgood.

Mr. Madison & Mr. Hamilton disapproved of these partial conventions, not as absolute violations of the Confederacy, but as ultimately leading to them & in the mean time exciting pernicious jealousies; the latter observing that he wished instead of them to see a General Convention take place & that he s^d^ soon in pursuance of intructions from his Constituents propose to Cong^s^ a plan for that purpose; the object w^d^ be to strengthen the fœderal Constitution.

Mr. White informed Cong^s^ that N. Hampshire had declined to accede to the plan of ~~a partial~~ the Convention on foot.

Mr. Higginson said that no Gentleman need be alarmed at any rate for it was pretty certain that the Convention would not take place. He wished with Mr. Hamilton to see a General Convention for the purpose of revising and amending the fœderal Government.

These observations having put an end to the subject, Cong^s^ resumed the Report on Revenue &c. Mr. Hamilton who had been absent when the last question was taken for substituting numbers in place of the value of land, moved to reconsider that vote. He was 2^ded^ by Mr. Osgood. See the Journal. Those who voted differently from their former votes were influenced by the conviction of the necessity of the change and despair on both sides of a more favorable rate of the slaves. The rate of $\frac{3}{5}$ was agreed to without opposition. On a preliminary question, the apportionm^t^ of the sum & revision of the same ref^d^ to Grand Com^e^

James Madison's Notes of Debates, concerning vote on valuation of slaves, April 1, 1783

The Report as to the Resignation of Foreign Ministers was taken up & on the case of Mr. Jefferson. See Journal. The Eastern delegates were averse to doing anything as to Mr. Adams untill further

A report from the Sec[y] of For: Affairs of a Treaty of Commerce to be entered into with G. Britain, was referred to Mr. Fitzsimmons, Mr. Higginson, Mr. Rutledge, Mr. Hemsley & Mr. Madison.

WEDNESDAY MAY 7.

The Resolution moved yesterday by Mr. Lee for indemnifying military Officers, being reported by the Committee, was agreed to.

The Committee on a motion of Mr. Dyer, reported "that the States which had settled with their respective lines of the Army for their pay since Aug. 1. 1780, should receive the securities which would otherwise be due to such lines."

The Report was opposed on the ground that the settlements had not been discharged in the value due. The Notes issued in payment by Connecticut were complained of, as being of little value.

The Report was disagreed to. See Journal.

THURSDAY MAY 8.

James Madison's Notes on Debates, May 8, 1783

Mr. Bland suggested that the Prisoners of War should be detained, until an answer be given as to the delivery of slaves, represented in a letter from Mr. Thomas Walke to be refused on the part of S[r] Guy Carleton.

On his motion seconded by Mr. Williamson it was ordered that the letter be sent to Gen: Washington for his information, in carrying into effect the Resolution of Ap[l] 15. touching arrangements with the British Commander for delivery of the posts, negroes &c.

A Portrait of Don Galvez was presented to Congress by Oliver Pollock.

FRIDAY MAY 9.

A question on a Report relating to the occupying the Posts when evacuated by the British was postponed by Virginia in right of a State.

Mr. Dyer moved a recommendation to the States to restore confiscated property conformably to the Provisional Articles. The motion produced a debate which went off without any positive result.

Adjourned to Monday.

MONDAY MAY 12.

See Journal.

TUESDAY MAY 13.

No Congress.

James Madison's Notes on Debates, concerning debate on discharging of troops, May 20 and May 23, 1783

Mr. Ellsworth enlarged on the impropriety of submitting to the Commander in Chief a point on which he could not possess competent materials for deciding. We ought either to discharge the men engaged for the war or to furlough them. He preferred the former.

Mr. Mercer descanted on the insidiousness of G. B., and warmly opposed the idea of laying ourselves at her mercy that we might save fifty thousand dollars; altho' Congress knew that they were violating the Treaty as to Negroes.

Mr. Williamson proposed that the Soldiers be furloughed. Mr. Carroll seconded him, that the two modes of furlough & discharge might both lye on the table.

By general consent this took place.

The Report as to confiscated property, on the Instructions from Virg^a^ & Penn^a^, was taken up, & agreed to be recommitted, together with a motion of Mr. Madison to provide for the case of Canadian refugees & for settlement of acc^ts^ with the British, and a motion of Mr. Hamilton to insert, in a definitive Treaty, a mutual stipulation not to keep a naval force on the Lakes.

WEDNESDAY MAY 21.
THURSDAY MAY 22.

See the Secret Journal for these two days.

The passage relating to the armed neutrality was generally concurred in for the reasons which it expresses.

The disagreements on the questions relating to a Treaty of Commerce with Russia were occasioned chiefly by sympathies, particularly in the Massachusetts Delegation with Mr. Dana; and by an eye in the navigating & Ship building States to the Russian Articles of Iron and Hemp. They were supported by S. Carolina, who calculated on a Russian market for her rice.

FRIDAY MAY 23.

The Report from Mr Hamilton, Mr Gorham and Mr Peters, in favor of discharging the soldiers enlisted for the war, was supported on the ground that it was called for by Economy and justified by the degree of certainty that the war would not be renewed. Those who voted for furloughing the soldiers wished to avoid expence, and at the same time to be not wholly unprepared for the contingent failure of a definitive treaty of peace. The view of the subject taken by those who were opposed both to discharging and furloughing, were explained in a motion by Mr. Mercer seconded by Mr. Izard to assign as reasons, first that Sr Guy Carleton had not given satisfactory reasons for continuing at N. York, second, that he had broken the Articles of the provisional Treaty relative to the negroes, by sending them off.

This motion appeared exceptionable to several, particularly to Mr. Hamilton & rather than it should be entered on the Journal by yeas & nays, it was agreed that the whole subject should lye over.

The Report relating to the Department of For. Affairs being taken up; Mr. Carroll seconded by Mr. Williamson moved that no public Minister should be employed by the U. S. except on extraordinary occasions.

In support of the proposition it was observed that it would not only be economical, but would withhold our distinguished Citizens from the corrupting scenes at foreign Courts, and what was of more consequence would prevent the residence of foreign Ministers in the U. S., whose intrigues & examples might be injurious both to the Gov[t] & to the people.

The considerations suggested on the other side were that Diplomatic relations made part of the established policy of modern civilized nations, that they tended to prevent hostile collisions by mutual & friendly explanations & that a young Republic ought not to incur the odium of so singular & as it might be thought disrespectful innovation. The discussion was closed by an Adjournment till Monday.

MONDAY MAY 26.

James Madison's Notes on Debates, May 26, 1783

The Resolutions on the Journal instructing the Ministers in Europe to remonstrate ag[st] the carrying off the Negroes; also those for furloughing the troops passed *unanimously*.

TUESDAY 27 MAY
WEDNESDAY 28 MAY } No Congress.

THURSDAY MAY 29.

The report of the Committee concerning Interest on British debts was committed, after some discussion.

FRIDAY MAY 30.

The debates on the Report recommending to the States a compliance with the 4th 5th & 6th of the provisional articles were renewed; the report being finally committed nem. con. See Secret Journal.

2. That in their persons, property and territory they shall be subject to the government of the United States in Congress assembled, and to the Articles of Confederation in all those cases in which the original States shall be so subject.

3. That they shall be subject to pay a part of the federal debts contracted or to be contracted to be apportioned on them by Congress according to the same common rule and measure, by which apportionments thereof shall be made on the other States.

4. That their respective governments shall be in republican forms, and shall admit no person to be a citizen who holds any hereditary title.

5. That after the year 1800 of the Christian era, there shall be neither slavery nor involuntary servitude in any of the said States, otherwise than in punishment of crimes, whereof the party shall have been duly convicted to have been personally guilty.

Committee report on resolutions concerning Northwest Territory, as read March 1, 1784

That whensoever any of the said States shall have, of free inhabitants as many as shall then be in any one the least numerous of the thirteen original States, such State shall be admitted by its Delegates into the Congress of the United States, on an equal footing with the said original States, after which the assent of two thirds of the United States in Congress assembled shall be requisite in all those cases, wherein by the Confederation, the assent of nine States is now required, provided the consent of nine States to such admission may be obtained according to the eleventh of the Articles of Confederation. Until such admission by their Delegates into Congress, any of the said States, after the establishment of their temporary government, shall have authority to keep a sitting member in Congress, with a right of debating, but not of voting.

That the Territory northward of the 45th degree, that is to say of the completion of 45° from the equator and ~~westward of Lake Superior~~ extending to the Lake of the Woods, shall be called **Sylvania**; that of the territory under the 45th and 44th degrees, that which lies westward of Lake Michigan shall be called **Michigania**; and that which is eastward thereof within the peninsula formed by the Lakes and waters of Michigan, Huron, St Clair and Erie shall be called **Cherronesus**, and shall include any part of the peninsula which may extend above the 45th degree. Of the territory under the 43d & 42d degrees, that to the westward thro' which the Assenisipi or Rock river runs shall be called **Assenisipia**; and that to the eastward in

Chase and Mr. [David] Howell, to whom was re-committed their report of a plan for a temporary government of the Western territory:

Motion and vote concerning Northwest Territory, April 19, 1784

When a motion was made by Mr. [Richard Dobbs] Spaight, seconded by Mr. [Jacob] Read, to strike out the following paragraph;

"That after the year 1800 of the Christian æra, there shall be neither slavery nor unvoluntary servitude in any of the said states, otherwise than in punishment of crimes whereof the party shall have been convicted to have been personally guilty:" And on the question, shall the words moved to be struck out stand the yeas and nays being required by Mr. [David] Howell,

State / Delegate	Vote	State vote
New Hampshire,		
Mr. Foster,	ay	ay
Blanchard,	ay	
Massachusetts,		
Mr. Gerry,	ay	ay
Partridge,	ay	
Rhode Island,		
Mr. Ellery,	ay	ay
Howell,	ay	
Connecticut,		
Mr. Sherman,	ay	ay
Wadsworth,	ay	
New York,		
Mr. De Witt,	ay	ay
Paine,	ay	
New Jersey,		
Mr. Dick,	ay	*
Pennsylvania,		
Mr. Mifflin,	ay	ay
Montgomery,	ay	
Hand,	ay	
Maryland,		
Mr. McHenry,	no	no
Stone,	no	
Virginia,		
Mr. Jefferson,	ay	no
Hardy,	no	
Mercer,	no	
North Carolina,		
Mr. Williamson,	ay	div.
Spaight,	no	
South Carolina,		
Mr. Read,	no	no
Beresford,	no	

So the question was lost, and the words were struck out.

The Delegates of N. York inform Congress that the Legislature of s^d State at their last session passed the following resolutions, Viz.

"*Resolved,* That the Delegates of this State be and they are hereby Instructed to Represent to the united States in Congress assembled that this State Deem it Essentially necessary to make Provision

Second. That ~~in their persons, property and territory~~ they shall be subject ~~to the government of the United States in Congress assembled and~~ to the Articles of Confederation in all those cases in which the original states shall be so subject, [and to all the acts and ordinances of the United States in Congress assembled, conformable thereto.

Third. That they in no case shall interfere with the primary disposal of the soil by the United states in Congress assembled, nor with the ordinances and regulations which Congress may find necessary, for securing the title in such soil to the bona fide purchasers.]

Fourth. That they shall be subject to pay a part of the federal debts contracted or to be contracted, to be apportioned on them by Congress, according to the same common rule and measure by which apportionments thereof shall be made on the other states.

Fifth. That no tax shall be imposed on lands, the property of the United States.

Sixth. That their respective governments shall be ~~in republican forms, and shall admit no person to be a citizen who holds any hereditary title. That after the year 1800 of the Christian era, there shall be neither slavery nor involuntary servitude in any of the said states, otherwise than in punishment of crimes, whereof the party shall have been convicted to have been personally guilty,~~ republican.

Resolution concerning the government of of Northwest Territory, as voted April 23, 1784. The black lines indicate words struck out by Congress

[Seventh. That the lands of non-resident proprietors shall, in no case, be taxed higher than those of residents within any new State, before the admission thereof to a vote by its delegates in Congress.]

That whensoever any of the said states shall have, of free inhabitants, as many as shall then be in any one the least numerous of the thirteen Original states, such State shall

Virginia,			*North Carolina,*		
Mr. Hardy,	no	no	Mr. Williamson,	ay	div.
Mercer,	no		Spaight,	no	
Monroe,	no		*South Carolina,*		
			Mr. Read,	no	no
			Beresford,	no	

So the question was lost.

Resolved, That the paragraph "That Consuls be appointed at the ports of   and Consuls General be established at   " be postponed till Saturday next.

The rest of the report being amended, was agreed to as follows:

Resolution, May 11, 1784

Resolved, That our said ministers to be Commissioned for treating with foreign nations, be referred to the instructions of the thirtieth day of May, 1783, relative to British debts, the objects of which they are hereby directed to urge with perseverance.

That they require with firmness and decision, full satisfaction for all slaves and other property belonging to citizens of these states taken and carried away in violation of the preliminary and definitive articles of peace; and to enable them to do this on precise grounds, Congress will furnish them with necessary facts and documents.

Resolved, That Doctor Franklin be desired to notify to the Apostolical Nuncio at Versailles, that Congress will always be pleased to testify their respect to his sovereign and state; but that the subject of his application to Doctor Franklin, being purely spiritual, it is without the jurisdiction and powers of Congress, who have no authority to permit or refuse it, these powers being reserved to the several states individually.

That Doctor Franklin be instructed to express to the Court of France the constant desire of Congress to meet

settlements of the citizens of the United States from the Indian villages and hunting grounds, and thereby extinguishing as far as possible all occasion for future animosity, disquiet and contention. That First, and as a preliminary, it shall be required, that all prisoners of whatever age or sex among the Indians, and all fugitive and other slaves shall be delivered up.

Committee report recommending resolutions concerning Indian affairs, as read May 28, 1784

Secondly, That the Indians be informed that after a contest of eight years for the sovereignty of this country, Great Britain has relinquished to the United States all claim to the country within the limits described by the second article of the definitive treaty between the United States and the King of Great Britain signed on the third day of September in the year 1783, that is to say (here insert the limits).

Thirdly. That as the Indians in contempt of every principle of justice and humanity regardless of the friendly temper and designs of the United States, and in defiance of their power or resentment, were determined to join their arms to those of Great Britain and to share her fortunes, so consequently by a less generous people than Americans they might be compelled to retire to the most distant parts of the Continent. But as we prefer clemency to rigour, as we persuade ourselves that their eyes are open to their error, and that they have found by fatal experience that their true interest and safety must depend upon our friendship, as the country is large enough to maintain and support us all, and as we are disposed to be Kind to them, to supply their wants, and to partake of their trade; we from these considerations and from motives of compassion, draw a veil over what is past, and will establish a boundary line between us and them beyond which we will restrain our citizens from hunting and settling, and within which the Indians shall not come but for the purposes of trading, treating, or other

of Indian affairs, dated Hillsborough June 4, 1784, beg leave to report the following draft of a letter to Gov[r] Martin to be signed by the Chairman of the Committee of the States:

ANNAPOLIS, *July 22, 1784.*

SIR,

Your letter dated Hillsborough July 4, 1784, to M[r] Beresford as Chairman of the Committee of Indian affairs, has been laid before the Committee of the States, from whom I have it in charge to inform you that Congress have not yet settled any Commission for Indian affairs in the Southern Department, and that the Committee of the States are not competent to accept of the goods mentioned in your letter, or to give any instructions relative to Treaties with the Indians in that Department. The whole of this business must therefore wait the decision of Congress at their next meeting. ~~In the name and in the behalf of the Committee of the States.~~

I have the honor to be &c.[1]

Resolution of Committee of the States, July 22, 1784

On the report of a committee, consisting of Mr. [Jacob] Read, Mr. [Hugh] Williamson and Mr. [Thomas] Stone, to whom was referred the letter signed T. Gilfillan, dated London, the 19th February, 1784, with the inspection roll of Negroes taken on board certain vessels at anchor near Staten Island, on the 30th day of November, 1783, signed T. Gilfillan and William Armstrong:

Resolved, That a copy of the said letter and roll be transmitted to the ministers plenipotentiary of the United States, for negotiating treaties with foreign powers, to be made use of in any negotiations they may have with the Court of Great Britain, agreeable to the instructions heretofore transmitted to them.[2]

On the report of a committee, consisting of Mr. [Hugh] Williamson, Mr. [Thomas] Stone and Mr. [Roger] Sher-

---

[1] This report, in the writing of Francis Dana, is in the *Papers of the Continental Congress*, No. 32, folio 7.

[2] This report, in the writing of Jacob Read, is in the *Papers of the Continental Congress*, No. 32, folio 81.

to any persons who may be now in possession the *bona fide* price, (where any has been given) which such persons may have paid on purchasing any of the said lands, rights or properties since the confiscation. And it is agreed that all persons who have any interest in confiscated lands, either by debts, marriage-settlements or otherwise, shall meet with no lawful impediment in the prosecution of their just rights.

"Art. 6th. That there shall be no future confiscations made, nor any prosecutions commenced against any person or persons, for or by reason of the part which he or they may have taken in the present war; and that no person shall, on that account, suffer any future loss or damage, either in his person, liberty or property, and that those who may be in confinement on such charges, at the time of the ratification of the treaty in America, shall be immediately set at liberty, and the prosecution so commenced be discontinued.

"Art. 7th. There shall be a firm and perpetual peace between his Britannic majesty and the said states, and between the subjects of the one, and the citizens of the other, wherefore all hostilities, both by sea and land, shall from henceforth cease; all prisoners on both sides shall be set at liberty, and his Britannic majesty shall, with all convenient speed, and without causing any destruction, or carrying away any Negroes or other property of the American inhabitants, withdraw all his armies, garrisons and fleets from the said United States, and from every post, place and harbour within the same; leaving in all fortifications the American artillery that may be therein, and shall also order and cause all archives, records, deeds and papers, belonging to any of the said states, or their citizens, which in the course of the war may have fallen into the hands of his officers, to be forthwith restored and delivered to the proper states and persons to whom they belong.

Treaty of peace with Great Britain, as read in Committee of the States, August 2, 1784

WEDNESDAY, JANUARY 26, 1785.

Congress assembled. Present, the same as yesterday.

On the report of a committee, consisting of Mr. [William] Ellery, Mr. [Samuel] Holten and Mr. [David] Williamson, to whom was referred a letter from the Secretary in the War Office, of the 20th January, 1785,

Resolved, That Michael Hillegas, esqr. continental treasurer, be directed to furnish Philip Audebert, deputy paymaster general, with the sum of three hundred and fifty nine dollars and forty two ninetieths of a dollar, being the amount of subsistence due to the officers in service for this present month of January, agreeably to an account enclosed in a letter of the Secy in the War Office to Congress, dated January 20, 1785.[1]

Also was read a letter from Nathanael Greene, regarding Capt. Finnie, dated January 25, 1785. It is in the *Papers of the Continental Congress,* No. 155, II, folio 702.

On this day, according to the indorsement, Mr. [Zephaniah] Platt was substituted for Mr. R. R. Livingston on the committee of December 20, 1784, on the letter from the Supreme Executive Council of Pennsylvania (President John Dickinson). See *post,* January 26, January 28 and February 11.

Also, according to indorsement, the letter from the Superintendent of Finance, dated January 15, 1782, on the establishment of a mint, was this day referred to the Grand Committee. This was the Grand Committee of January 17, with a few changes in personnel, which, was renewed, according to Committee Book No. 186, on April 6.

[1] The report, in the writing of William Ellery, is in the *Papers of the Continental Congress,* No. 27, folio 271. Secretary Carleton's letter is in No. 60, folio 115.

On this day, as the indorsement states, was read a petition of Edward Antill for relief from depreciation of his pay, and referred to Mr. [David] Howell, Mr. [Hugh] Williamson and Mr. [Pierse] Long. It is in No. 42, I, folio 75. According to Committee Book No. 190, a report was made March 9 and Committee Book, No. 191, shows that the committee report was transferred; the indorsement on the petition states that it was filed September 19, 1786.

Also a petition of Michael Byrne for Congress's patronage of his invention which was reported on by the Committee of the Week and ordered to lie. It is in No. 42, I, folio 335.

Receipt of address, January 26, 1785

Also, an address, signed by appointment, of a meeting of Quakers pleading for the abolition of negro slavery. It is in No. 43, folio 347.

Also, on this or an approximate date, a memorial of James Duane and Walter Livingston, agents for New York, protesting against holding a federal court to

and Territories within their Limits, which are now held ~~against them~~ by british Garrisons. And you will take the earliest opportunity of transmitting the answer you may receive to this Requisition.

~~You will endeavour to make yourself acquainted with the Disposition of the british Cabinet to join with the United States in proper pacific measures for inducing Spain to cease opposing the free navigation of the Missisippi; and to that end a Display of the commercial advantages which would flow to them through that Channel, would probably prove a powerful Inducement.~~

You will remonstrate against the Infraction of the Treaty of Peace by the Exportation of Slaves and other american Property, contrary to the Stipulations on that Subject in the   article of it. Upon this Head you will be supplied with various authentic Papers and Documents, perticularly the Correspondence between General Washington and others on the one Part, and Sir Guy Carlton on the other.

Report of instructions to ministers to Great Britain, as read February 7, 1785

You will represent to the british Ministry the strong and necessary Tendency of their Restrictions on our Trade, to incapacitate our merchants in a certain Degree, to make Remittances to theirs.

~~You will so manage your Conferences with the Minister on the Subject of Commerce, as to discover whether he is inclined to make a Treaty with us and on what Terms, taking care not to enter into any Engagements without the previous approbation of Congress.~~

You will represent in Strong Terms the Losses which many of our and also of their merchants will sustain if the former be unseasonably and immoderately pressed for the payment of Debts contracted before the war; ~~and (if compliance should appear probable) you will solicit the Interposition and Influence of Government to prevent it.~~ On this Subject you will be furnished with Papers in which it is amply discussed.[1]

[1] This draft, in the writing of John Jay, is in the *Papers of the Continental Congress*, No. 25, II, folio 407. According to the indorsement it was read this day and passed March 7.

February 7: The following committees were appointed: Of the Week—Mr. [William] Houstoun, Mr. [Zephaniah] Platt and Mr. [Joseph] Gardner. Mr. [David] Howell, Mr. [John] Bull and Mr. [John] Henry, on the Memorial of John Story and letter from Nathanael Greene on depreciation and pay while settling accounts. They reported April 26. A report of the Board of Treasury on Story's memorial was rendered, February 1, 1788.

Mr. [Hugh] Williamson, Mr. [Elbridge] Gerry, Mr. [Rufus] King, Mr. [David] Howell and Mr. [William Samuel] Johnson, on the memorial of Moses Hazen on dispute with John Pierce over settling Hazen's accounts. Mr. S[amuel] Holten

(as the case may be) vizt 1 Certificate dated N^o pay^s to and amounting to &c.[1]

The Committee consisting of Mr. [Samuel] Hardy, Mr. [William] Houston, Mr. [Jacob] Read, Mr. [Hugh] Williamson and Mr. [Samuel] Holten, to whom was referred the Report of a Committee on the State of SOUTHERN INDIAN AFFAIRS, beg leave to submit the following Report:

That commissioners, with the same pay that is allowed the commissioners for treating with the northern Indians, be immediately appointed to form a treaty or treaties with the Indians in the southern department, for the purpose of making peace with them, receiving them into the favor of the United States, and ascertaining the boundary lines by which the settlements of the citizens of the United States are or ought to be separated and divided from the Indian villages and hunting grounds; and thereby if possible extinguishing animosity, and preventing in future any contention or disquiet.

That the southern department be considered as extending so far north as to include the Cherokees, and so far south as to include all the other nations or tribes of Indians who reside within the limits of the United States, or have been at war with them, or any of them.

Committee report, as submitted March 4, 1785

1. That the commissioners be instructed as a preliminary, to require that all prisoners of whatever age or sex among the Indians, and all slaves or other fugitives, shall be delivered up.

2. That the Indians be informed that their former ally the king of Great Britain unprovoked, waged a cruel and bloody war against the United States; that he equipped and sent forth powerful fleets upon our coasts to destroy our trade, and great armies amongst us to waste our country; but that after a conflict of eight years, during which two of those armies were defeated and captured, Great Britain has been compelled to relinquish to the United States, by a treaty which was signed on the 3d of September, 1783, all claim to that vast country which is included between St. Croix and St. Mary's rivers, and between the ocean and the great lakes; that is to say, (here describe the bounds according to the 2d article in the treaty of peace.) That

[1] This report, in the writing of Elbridge Gerry, is in the *Papers of the Continental Congress*, No. 26, folio 513. Committee Book No. 190 states that the report was made March 4. The indorsement of the report says that it was read March 5, Wednesday 9 March assigned for consideration and 19 Sept. 1786 filed. Committee Book No. 191 states that it was referred to the Grand Committee.

Congress took into consideration a report of the Secretary for Foreign Affairs; and thereupon agreed to the following

INSTRUCTIONS

For a Minister Plenipotentiary appointed to represent the United States of America at the Court of Great Britain.

Sir,

You will in a respectful but firm manner insist, that the United States be put without further delay in possession of all the posts and territories within their limits which are now held by British Garrisons: and you will take the earliest opportunity of transmitting the answer you may receive to this requisition.

Instructions, as agreed upon March 7, 1785

You will remonstrate against the infraction of the treaty of peace by the exportation of negroes and other American property, contrary to the stipulations on that subject in the Seventh Article of it. Upon this head you will be supplied with various authentick papers and documents, particularly the correspondence between General Washington and others on the one part, and Sir Guy Carleton on the other.

You will represent to the British Ministry the strong and necessary tendency of their restrictions on our trade to incapacitate our Merchants in a certain degree to make remittances to theirs.

You will represent in strong terms the losses which many of our and also of their Merchants will sustain, if the former be unseasonably and immoderately pressed for the payment of debts contracted before the war. On this subject you will be furnished with papers, in which it is amply discussed.[1]

[1] These instructions were also entered in the manuscript Secret Journal, Foreign Affairs, No. 5, and in Secret Journal No. 4. A copy is in Secret Journal No. 6, Vol. III.

Committee report concerning the appointment of commissioners to make peace with Southern Indians, as submitted March 11, 1785

That the commissioners be instructed as a preliminary, to require that all prisoners of whatever age or sex among the Indians, shall be delivered up and they are further instructed to demand the negroes and other property belonging to the Citizens of the U. S. which have been captured during the war.

That they be instructed to inform the Indians of the great occurrences of the last war and of the extent of Country relinquished by the late treaty of Peace with G. B.

That the commissioners previous to their holding any treaty, shall give due notice of the time and place where it is to be held, to the supreme executives of Virginia N. Carolina, So. C. and G., in order that they may each of them appoint one or more persons to attend during the treaty if they think proper.

That the commissioners be instructed to encourage the Indians to give notice to Congress, or some of their officers, of any designs that may be formed in any neighbouring tribe, or by any person whatever against the peace of the United States.

That the Commissioners be authorized to ~~draw upon the~~ apply to the supream Executive ~~either~~ of Virg^{a} North Carolina or South Carolina or Georgia for 150 men or such part thereof as they may deem necessary of their Militia for the purpose of protecting the Commissioners whilst engaged in concluding the s^{d} treaties; and that they be authorized to ~~call on~~ draw on ~~either~~ any of the said States and draw for the same on the Comm^{rs} of the treasury who are hereby directed to pay such Draft ~~for dollars to enable them to procure such goods for the purpose of making presents as shall be necessary to carry such treaty into effect~~ and that ~~such~~ the said state have credit for such advance out of the requisitions for the year 1786 ~~in addition to~~ and also the amount of the goods purchased as above.

That Monday next be assigned for the appointm^{t} of three Commissioners to form a treaty or treaties with the Indians in the southern department agreeable to the foregoing ~~resolution~~ report and for the purposes specified in the same.[1]

[1] This report, in the writing of Charles Thomson, on the printed report of March 4, and the last two paragraphs in the writing of Samuel Hardy and William Houstoun, respectively, is in the *Papers of the Continental Congress*, No. 30, folios 247 and 245½ and 254. The provision for drawing on the Commissioners of the Treasury to meet the treaty expense is in the writing of Thomson on a vote, presumably taken during the debate on this report, folio 254. As amended during the debate, the report was finally adopted March 15. The commissioners were appointed March 21.

for treating with the Northern Indians, be appointed to treat with the Cherokees and all other Indians southward of them, within the limits of the United States, or who have been at War with them, for the purpose of making Peace with them, receiving them into the favour and protection of the United States, and removing as far as may be all causes of future contention or quarrels.

That the commissioners be instructed as a preliminary, to require that all prisoners of whatever age or sex among the Indians, shall be delivered up, and they are further instructed to demand the Negroes and other property belonging to the Citizens of the United States, which have been captured during the War.

Resolution concerning the appointment of commissioners to make peace with Southern Indians, March 15, 1785

That they be instructed to inform the Indians of the great occurrences of the last War, and of the extent of Country relinquished by the late treaty of peace with Great Britain.

That the Commissioners, previous to their holding any Treaty, shall give due notice of the time and place where it is to be held, to the Supreme Executives of Virginia, North Carolina, South Carolina and Georgia; in order that they may each of them appoint one or more persons to attend during the Treaty, if they think proper.

That the Commissioners be instructed to encourage the Indians to give notice to Congress or some of their Officers, of any designs that may be formed in any neighbouring tribe, or by any person whatever against the peace of the United States.

That the Commissioners be authorised to apply to the Supreme Executive of Virginia, North Carolina, South Carolina or Georgia, for one hundred and fifty men, or such part thereof as they may deem necessary of their Militia, for the purpose of protecting the Commissioners whilst engaged in concluding the said Treaties; and that they be authorised to draw on any

That the Petition of the Officers of the late American Regiment, stating that Doctor Heart the Surgeon of their Regit had received,

P. on an order from the paymaster General a Sum of Money for the Regimental paymaster, to be applied to the subsistance of the said officers, that on the return of Doctor Heart from Boston and in the absence of the paymaster, they with the approbation of the Doctor distributed to each officer six weeks pay, and gave receipts for so much, as if received of the regimental paymaster which receipts they pray, after considering all the circumstances of their situation and distress, may be allowed by the Comptroller as vouchers to the pay master for the said six weeks pay, be referred to a Committee.

That the petition of William Adams praying for a compensation

P. for his losses by the enemy he entered on the files

[1] WEDNESDAY, MARCH 16, 1785.

Proposition and vote concerning Northwest Territory, March 16, 1785

Congress assembled. Present as yesterday.

A motion was made by Mr. [Rufus] King, seconded by Mr. [William] Ellery, that the following proposition be committed.

That there shall be neither Slavery nor involuntary servitude in any of the States, described in the resolve of Congress of the 23 April, 1784, otherwise than in punishment of crimes, whereof the party shall have been personally guilty: And that this regulation shall be an article of compact, and remain a fundamental principle of the Constitutions between the 13 Original States, and each of the States described in the said resolve of the 23 April, 1784.[2]

On the question for commitment, the yeas and nays being required by Mr. [Rufus] King,

[1] At this point the entries are resumed by Charles Thomson.

[2] This motion, in the writing of Rufus King, is in the *Papers of the Continental Congress*, No. 31, folio 327. The indorsement states that it was referred to Mr. [Rufus] King, Mr. [David] Howell and Mr. [William] Ellery, who reported, according to Committee Book No. 190, on April 6.

State	Member	Vote	State vote
New Hampshire,			
	Mr. Foster,	ay	ay
	Long,	ay	
Massachusetts,			
	Mr. Holten,	ay	ay
	King,	ay	
Rhode Island,			
	Mr. Ellery,	ay	ay
	Howell,	ay	
Connecticut,			
	Mr. Cook,	ay	ay
	Johnson,	ay	
New York,			
	Mr. W. Livingston,	ay	ay
	Platt,	ay	
New Jersey,			
	Mr. Beatty,	ay	ay
	Cadwallader,	ay	
	Stewart,	ay	
Pennsylvania,			
	Mr. Gardner,	ay	ay
	W. Henry,	ay	
Maryland,			
	Mr. M'Henry,	no	ay
	J. Henry,	ay	
	Hindman,	ay	
Virginia,			
	Mr. Hardy,	no	no
	Lee,	no	
	Grayson,	ay	
North Carolina,			
	Mr. Spaight,	no	no
	Sitgreaves,	no	
South Carolina,			
	Mr. Bull,	no	no
	Pinckney,	no	
Georgia,			
	Mr. Houstoun,	no	*

So it was resolved in the affirmative.

Congress proceeded to the election of a Commissioner for carrying into execution the purposes mentioned in the Ordinance of the 23 Decr, 1784, in the room of Philip Schuyler, Esqr who has declined; and, the ballots being taken, Mr. John Brown was elected, having been previously nominated by Mr. [John] Beatty.

The ordinance for ascertaining the mode of locating and disposing of lands in the Western territory, being taken up for a second reading; after debate,

Ordered, That it be referred to a comee of a member from each State.[1]

[1] On this day also, according to Committee Book No. 190, Mr. [Pierse] Long, Mr. [Rufus] King, Mr. [David] Howell, Mr. [William Samuel] Johnson, Mr. R. R. Livingston, Mr. [Archibald] Stewart, Mr. [Joseph] Gardner, ~~Mr. W. Henry,~~ Mr. J[ohn] Henry, Mr. [William] Grayson, Mr. [Hugh] Williamson, Mr. [John] Bull and Mr. [William] Houstoun, were appointed to prepare an ordinance for locating lands in the Western territory. They reported April 12.

Committee report on resolution concerning Northwest Territory, as submitted April 6, 1785

The Committee consisting of &c. [Mr. Rufus King, Mr. David Howell and Mr. William Ellery] to whom was referred a motion from Mr King for the exclusion of Involuntary servitude in the States described in the Resolve of Congress of the 23d day of April, 1784, submit the following Resolve—

Resolved, That after the year 1800 of the christian Era there shall be neither slavery nor involuntary servitude in any of the states described in the Resolve of Congress of the 23d day of April 1784, otherwise than in punishment of crimes whereof the party shall have been personally guilty, and that this Regulation shall be an Article of Compact, and remain a fundamental principle of the constitutions between the 13 original states, and each of the states described in the said Resolve of Congress of the 23d day of April 1784, any implication or construction of the said Resolve to the contrary notwithstanding—Provided always, that upon the escape of any person into any of the states described in the said Resolve of Congress of the 23d Day of Apl. 1784, from whom labor or service is lawfully claimed in any one of the 13 origl states, such fugitive may be lawfully reclaimed, and carried back to the person claiming his labor or service as aforesaid this Resolve notwithstanding.[1]

THURSDAY, APRIL 7, 1785.

Congress assembled. Present, New Hampshire, Massachusetts, Rhode Island, Connecticut, New York, New Jersey, Pennsylvania, Delaware, Virginia, and South Carolina; and from North Carolina, Mr. [Hugh] Williamson.

On motion of Mr. [Melancton] Smith,

Resolved, That the determination of the question which was yesterday postponed by the state of Rhode Island, be further postponed till to Morrow.

Congress resumed the Consideration of the report on the motions relative to the western frontiers, and a motion being made by Mr. [David] Howell, seconded by Mr. [John] Beatty,

[1] This report, in the writing of Rufus King, is in the *Papers of the Continental Congress,* No. 31, folio 329. The indorsement states that it was read on this day and Thursday April 14 assigned for consideration. A printed copy is on folio 331, indorsed by Thomson: "To prevent slavery in the new states. Included in substance in the Ordinance for a temporary government of western territory passed the 13 July, 1787."

the said Officers and Soldiers, and persons claiming under them, the lands they are entitled to, agreeably to the said deed of cession, and Act of Congress accepting the same.

And on the question to agree to this amendment, the yeas and nays being required by the Delegates of Maryland,

New Hampshire,			*Maryland,*		
Mr. Foster,	ay	ay	Mr. McHenry,	no	no
Long,	ay		J. Henry,	no	
Massachusetts,			Hindman,	no	
Mr. Holten,	ay	ay	*Virginia,*		
King,	ay		Mr. Monroe,	ay	ay
Rhode Island,			Lee,	ay	
Mr. Ellery,	ay	ay	Grayson,	ay	
Howell,	ay		*North Carolina,*		
Connecticut,			Mr. Williamson,	ay	ay
Mr. Johnson,	ay	*	Sitgreaves,	ay	
New York,			*South Carolina,*		
Mr. Lawrance,	ay	ay	Mr. Pinckney,	ay	*
Smith,	ay		*Georgia,*		
Pennsylvania,			Mr. Houstoun,	ay	*
Mr. Gardner,	ay	ay			
Wilson,	ay				

So it was resolved in the affirmative.

On this day, according to the indorsement, the letter from William Winder, Commissioner for settling the accounts of the State of Delaware, dated March 17, which had been referred to a committee March 23, was referred to the Board of Treasury which reported May 13. See *post*, May 23.

Also, according to Committee Book No. 190, the committee of January 24 on Canadian claims was, this day, discharged of the claim of Laurent Olivier and an indorsement on the Lee motion above notes that "they [the papers in the Canadian claims were] deliver'd to the persons upon application." See *ante*, March 9.

Reading of a letter from George Washington, April 28, 1785

On this day also, according to the indorsement was read a letter from the Secretary for Foreign Affairs, dated April 27, enclosing a letter from George Washington dated April 5, to Charles Thomson respecting negroes carried away by the British from New York city in 1783 and enclosing also a letter from Thomson to Secretary Jay, dated April 22, relative to the same matter. Jay's letter is in the *Papers of the Continental Congress*, No. 80, I, folio 145. Washington's letter is entered in the Washington Letter Books, No. 6, p. 63.

April 28: The following committees were appointed: Mr. [William Samuel] Johnson, Mr. [Rufus] King, Mr. J[ohn] Henry, Mr. [Charles] Pinckney, Mr. [John] Lawrence, Mr. [James] Monroe and Mr. [William] Grayson, on the letter

On a report of the board of treasury, on a memorial of Hendrick Smock, and of Increase Carpenter,

Resolved, That in all cases where certificates of the United States payable to the bearer, have been lost, and no satisfactory evidence given of the same having been destroyed, it would be improper that any new certificates should issue to replace the same.

That Increase Carpenter produce to the loan Officer of the State where the said certificates issued, the fragments of the certificates by him preserved, being No. two thousand four hundred and twenty seven, one thousand dollars; No. three thousand six hundred and fifteen, two hundred dollars; and No. seven thousand five hundred and eighty seven, Four hundred dollars; and in case the loan officer shall be satisfied of the authenticity of the fragments to him produced, he is hereby authorised and directed, to issue new certificates of the same tenor and date as those destroyed.

Resolution,
August 19, 1785

Motion on a letter of 27. April, 1785, from Secy for Foreign Affairs]

Resolved, That the Secretary for foreign Affairs be directed to employ some person ~~to go to Genl Washington for the purpose of transcribing and bringing to Congress~~ to collect from Genl Washington a list of the Negroes carryed off from New York by the British Army, or others in violation of the late treaty of peace; to the end that our Minister at the Court of London may be furnished with a Copy of the said list as early as possible.[1]

[Motion of Mr. Elbridge Gerry]

That after the 1st Monday of Novr next all Directions to Congress shall be addressed to their Excellencies the President and Members of the U. States in Congress assembled.

That each Member of Congress shall take Rank of every officer of the U. States.

[1] This motion, in the writing of Samuel Hardy, is in the *Papers of the Continental Congress,* No. 36, III, folio 107. The indorsement states that it was referred to the Secretary for Foreign Affairs to take order. It is also entered, with the order, in Resolve Book No. 123, p. 34.

April 4.

Reports on letter of Cyrus Griffin and John Lowell; Petition of Joseph Ellis and case of Daniel Darby.

466. (1) The Committee to whom were referred a Letter of the of / December from the honorable Cyrus Griffin and John Lowell, Esquires, / Judges of the Court of Appeals, and a Motion of Mr. Howell's, Re - / port, /

(2) The Committee to whom was referred the Petition of Joseph / Ellis, praying a re-hearing in the Case of the Sloop Hannah, condemned / in the Court of Admiralty of the State of New-Jersey, a Reversal of which / Decree was obtained before the Judges of Appeal; together with a Re- / port of the Secretary of Foreign Affairs, in the Case between Daniel Darby, / qui tam, Appellant, and the Imperial Brig Ersten and her Cargo, Pd. / Thomson, Master, &c. beg leave to recommend that it be / Resolved, / F°. Broadside.

A copy is in the Library of Congress. It measures 42.8 x 26.5 cms. From Dunlap's press, run off April 6 in an edition of 60 copies. *Papers of the Continental Congress*, No. 146, Register of Accounts.

April 6.

Report on Slavery in new States.

List of documents, April 6, 1785

467. The Committee consisting of, &c. to whom was refer- / red a Motion of Mr. King, for the Exclusion of invo- / luntary Servitude in the States described in the Resolve of Con- / gress of the 23d Day of April, 1784, submit the following / Resolve. 4°. Broadside.

A copy is in the Library of Congress. It measures 26.5 x 21.2 cms. Another copy in the *Papers of the Continental Congress*, No. 31, folio 331, bears the following indorsement by Charles Thomson: "To prevent slavery in the new states. Included in substance in the Ordinance for a temporary government of western territory passed the 13 July 1787." From the press of John Dunlap, an edition of 60 copies, run off April 11. *Papers of the Continental Congress*, No. 146, Register of Accounts.

April 12.

Ordinance for disposing of lands in the Western Territory.

468. An Ordinance for ascertaining the Mode of disposing of Lands / in the Western Territory. / F°. Broadside.

A copy is in the Library of Congress. It is in double column and measures 42.7 x 26.7 cms. See Journals, April 15. This imprint seems to be the re-committed Ordinance noted in the Journals of April 14 as read the *first* time. From the press of John Dunlap, an edition of 100 copies, run off April 15. *Papers of the Continental Congress*, No. 146,

The Committee consisting of Mr. [Nathan] Dane, Mr. [William] Grayson, Mr. [Stephen Mix] Mitchel, Mr. [James] Monroe and Mr. [John] Kean to whom was referred the motion of Mr. Dane of Feb[y] 27, 1786, report:

That they have carefully attended to the several matters referred to them, and on examining the doings of Congress and the several States relative thereto, find, that Congress, at an early period in the affairs of the Union, having no federal rule for apportioning taxes and the common charges of the Confederacy on the respective States, established by them, adopted as the only one in their power, in any degree practicable, the number of Inhabitants in each State, with some small variations, that the necessities and wants of the late war rendered indispensable.

When the articles of Confederation and perpetual union between the States came under their examination, and the consideration of Congress; and particularly the 8th article of it, the inequalities and difficulties that would attend the carrying of it into effect, were foreseen by several of the States, and therefore this part of the federal Compact was, then, in a peculiar manner, objected to. These difficulties then but imperfectly foreseen and stated have, by many years experience, been sufficiently realized and fully demonstrated; for Notwithstanding 5 years have elapsed since this compact was finally ratified; and Notwithstanding the earnest Recommendation of Congress to the several States, passed more than three years ago, to make and transmit to the United States in Congress, an accurate, and Just account of the quantity of land in each State, with the buildings and improvements thereon, according to the tenor of that article; yet, not a single State in the Union has, in any degree, complied therewith, and transmitted such account; unless an unauthenticated account transmitted by the State of New Hampshire of the houses, other buildings and lands in that State, a part whereof was imperfectly formed ~~from conjecture~~ can be considered a compliance. But about the same time, that Congress, lest no other federal rule of apportionment should be adopted by the States, recommended the carrying that article into execution, Congress appears to have been aware of the impracticability in some degree of its execution, and the inequality of its operation; for the U. States in Congress assembled on the 18th of April, 1783, after mature deliberation, and examining the subject in its full extent, almost unanimously agreed to propose to the States an alteration of that article; and instead of the rule of

Committee report on taxation, March 8, 1786

apportionment therein prescribed, to adopt the rule, then proposed, of supplying the common Treasury in proportion to the number of white and other free Citizens and inhabitants, and three fifths of all other persons, Indians not paying taxes excepted, as a more convenient and certain rule of assertaining the proportion to be supplied by the respective States; to be triennially taken in such mode as Congress should direct and appoint.

The reasons that induced the federal Government, at the time, to recommend this constitutional alteration of the Confederacy, the Justice, propriety, and expediency of the change, are fully and largely stated to the several Legislatures in the address of Congress to them of the same month of April; to which Congress again ought, in the opinion of this Committee, in the most pressing manner to call their earliest attention.

In examining the several laws passed by the States in pursuance of the above recommendation, the Committee find, that a majority of the States, and a great proportion of the whole confederacy, have readily and fully approved of the proposed alteration of that article of the federal Government; that nine States, including ~~the largest in the Union have~~ Massachusetts, Connecticut, New York, New Jersey, Pennsylvania, Delaware, Maryland, Virginia, and North Carolina, have, by their legislative acts, passed in pursuance of said recommendation, fully complied with it, and authorised the respective Delegates in Congress to ratify the alteration proposed. But they do not find that the other States have passed any laws, or taken any measures on the subject; nor do they find that any well founded exceptions or any particular objection has been made by those States, to the plan proposed; it is to be observed that the power of appointing in what mode the number of Inhabitants in each State, shall be so ascertained and transmitted, is vested in the federal Government, by the act of Congress and those laws passed by several States and it is thereby the duty of that Government to direct the same; But it does not appear that Congress has taken any measures for that purpose; or that any State has so taken and transmitted the number of its inhabitants in consequence of that recommendation. In February and March, 1782, March, 1783, and November, 1784, it appears the States of Rhode Island, Connecticut, New Jersey, and Maryland, returned to Congress the number of their inhabitants, respectively, distinguishing white from black; but as these returns are not founded on the principles of the said Recommendation, nor

they have been accustomed to in fixing, from time to time, this value. An interested discretion must decide on questions on which the existence of the Union may depend. It can require but little discernment to foresee that the Judgment of men will be biassed continually by interest and local connexions, and such are their dispositions, that States will, on every occasion, suspect each other of partiality; the consequence of which will be, differences, disputes, and animosities among them.

The Committee have carefully attended to some objections to the proposed alteration, said to prevail in some of the States—that it must operate unequally, and to the disadvantage of some particular States; and that the taking of three-fifths of all other persons therein mentioned is not bringing a sufficient number of that Class of people into the estimate; but they do not find that those objections are founded on any particular calculations or documents. As to the last objection, it may be observed, that there is no possible rule by which the acquisitions and abilities of freemen can be accurately compared with that of persons who are in a State of servitude; but few can doubt, that the acquisitions and abilities of freemen, capable of directing their own conduct, and moved to exersions by motives founded on their own immediate interest, are much superior to those of Slaves, whose actions have no other Spring than the interest and directions of a master; but on a question so uncertain, and not very extensive in its effects, it is to be ardently wished that a disposition to make mutual concessions will be continued and promoted through all the States so intimately concerned in one great and one Common Interest; and as to the objections, that the proposed substitute will have a more unequal effect than the present federal rule, is, in the opinion of the Committee, a matter very questionable; or that it will operate to the disadvantage of some States, is a point by no means established. As there is no rule in this Case by which federal taxes can be assessed, and but little probability the States will put in operation the one in the Confederation, in its present form, but may soon be induced to adopt the proposed alteration, the Committee are of opinion, that the States, which have not acceded to that alteration be again earnestly called upon to do it; and that it be recommended to all the States immediately to take effectual measures for ascertaining and transmitting to the United States in Congress assembled the number of Inhabitants in each State, making the proper distinctions and lest that alteration shall not finally be adopted, and Congress shall be constrained to carry intoo peration the federal, rule of apportionment heretofore acceded to by the several States[that it be also again recommended to the States to pursue effectual measures for obtaining the object of the resolve of February 17, 1783, relative to this subject; for, however exceptionable the federal rule in this Case may be in its present form as to its execution and effects, yet, it is the only one acceded to by the States, and if no other rule can be agreed to by them, the Common charges of the union must, and ought to be, apportioned on it and if the several States do not very speedily transmit to Congress the proper materials whereon to form a federal rule of apportionment it will become the indispensable duty of Congress to execute the rule of the Confederation in the best manner in their power, and when they have so done they must stand excused from any injustice or inequality that may take place. Therefore the Committee submit the following resolves:

Resolved, That it be earnestly recommended to the Legislature of the States of New Hampshire, Rhode Island, and Providence plantations, ~~Delaware~~ South Carolina, and Georgia, to take into their immediate consideration the said recommendation of Congress of April 18, 1783, so far as it respects the alteration of the eighth of the articles of Confederation and perpetual union between the States, and to authorise their Delegates, respectively in Congress, to subscribe and ratify the proposed alteration of it.

Resolved, That it be recommended to the Legislatures of the several States immediately to pass laws, and to take the most effectual measures for ascertaining and transmitting to the United States in Congress assembled on or before the first day of July next, the number of white and other free inhabitants of every age, sex, and condition, in their respective States, including those bound to servitude for terms of years, and the number of all other persons not comprehended in the foregoing description except Indians not paying taxes in each State, and for ascertaining and transmitting the like number in like manner triennually forever hereafter.

Resolved, That it be again recommended to the Legislatures of the several States to take into their consideration the said Resolve of

91716°—vol 30—34——8

the Commissioners plenipotentiary of the United States of America, of the one part, and the Chiefs and Warriors of the Shawanoe Nation of the other part.

Treaties with the Cherokees, Chickasaws, and Choctaws, as entered in the Journal, April 17, 1786

Art. 1st. Three hostages shall be immediately delivered to the Commissioners, to remain in the possession of the United States, until all the prisoners, white and black, taken in the late war from among the citizens of the United States, by the Shawanoe nation, or by any other Indian or Indians residing in their towns, shall be restored.

Art. 2d. The Shawanoe nation, do acknowledge the United States to be the sole and absolute sovereigns of all the territory ceded to them by a treaty of peace, made between them and the King of Great Britain, the fourteenth day of January, one thousand seven hundred and eighty-four.

Art. 3d. If any Indian or Indians of the Shawanoe nation, or any other Indian or Indians residing in their towns, shall commit murder or robbery on, or do any injury to the Citizens of the United States, or any of them, that nation shall deliver such offender, or offenders, to the Officer commanding the nearest post of the United States, to be punished according to the Ordinances of Congress: And in like manner any citizen of the United States who shall do an Injury to any Indian of the Shawanoe nation, or to any other Indian or Indians residing in their towns, and under their protection, shall be punished according to the laws of the United States.

Art. 4th. The Shawanoe nation having knowledge of the intention of any nation or body of Indians to make war on the citizens of the United States, or of their counselling together for that purpose, and neglecting to give information thereof to the commanding officer of the nearest post of the United States, shall be considered as parties in such war, and be punished accordingly; and the United States shall in like manner inform the Shawanoes of any injury designed against them.

Art. 5th. The United States do grant peace to the Shawanoe nation, and do receive them into their friendship and protection.

Art. 6th. The United States do allot to the Shawanoe nation, lands within their territory to live and hunt upon, beginning at the South line of the lands allotted to the Wiandots and Delaware nations, at the place where the main branch of the great Miami which falls into the Ohio intersects said line; then down the river Miami, to the fork of that river, next below the old fort, which was taken by the French in 1752; thence due west to the river de la Panse; then down that

states on the one part, and all the Cherokees on the other, shall be universal; and the contracting parties shall use their utmost endeavours to maintain the peace given as aforesaid, and friendship re-established.

In witness of all, and every thing herein determined, between the United States of America, and all the Cherokees: We their underwritten commissioners, by virtue of our full powers have signed this definitive treaty, and have caused our seals to be hereunto affixed. Done at Hopewell, on the Keowee, this 28th of November, in the year of our Lord one thousand seven hundred and eighty five.

(Signed:) Benjamin Hawkins, Andrew Pickens, Joseph Martin, Lachn. M'Intosh, and by thirty seven head men of the Cherokee Nation.

Articles of a treaty, concluded at Hopewell, on the Keowee river, near Seneca old town, between Benjamin Hawkins, Andrew Pickens and Joseph Martin, Commissioners plenipotentiary of the United States of America of the one part, and Piomingo, Head Warrior and first Minister of the Chickasaw Nation, Mingatushka, one of the leading chiefs, and Latopoia, first beloved man of the said nation;[1] Commissioners Plenipotentiary of all the Chickasaws of the other part.

The Commissioners plenipotentiary of the United States of America, give peace to the Chickasaw nation, and receive them into the favour and protection of the said States, on the following conditions:

Article 1. The Commissioners plenipotentiary of the Chickasaw Nation, shall restore all the prisoners, Citizens of the United States, to their entire liberty, if any there be in the Chickasaw Nation. They shall also restore all the Negroes, and all other property taken during the late War, from the Citizens, if any there be in the Chickasaw Nation, to such person, and at such time and place, as the Commissioners of the United States of America shall appoint.

Article 2d. The Commissioners plenipotentiary of the Chickasaws, do hereby acknowledge the tribes and the towns of the Chickasaw Nation, to be under the protection of the United States of America, and of no other Sovereign whosoever.

Article 3d. The boundary of the lands hereby allotted to the Chickasaw Nation to live and hunt on, within the limits of the United States of America, is, and shall be the following, viz:

[1] At this point Benjamin Bankson commences the entry in the Journal.

Articles of a treaty concluded at Hopewell, on the Keowee, near Seneca old town, between Benjamin Hawkins, Andrew Pickens and Joseph Martin, Commissioners plenipotentiary of the United States of America of the one part; and Yockonahoma, great medal Chief of Soonacoha, Yockahoopoia, leading Chief of Bugtoogoloo, Mingohoopoie, leading Chief of Haskooqua, Tobocoh, great medal Chief of Congaloo, Pooshemastubie, gorget Captain of Sonayazo, and thirteen small medal chiefs of the first class, twelve medal and gorget captains, Commissioners plenipotentiary, of all the Chocktaw Nation of the other part.

The Commissioners plenipotentiary of the United States of America give peace to all the Choctaw nation, and receive them into the favour and protection of the United States of America, on the following conditions:

Article 1st. The Commissioners plenipotentiary of all the Choctaw Nation, shall restore all the prisoners, citizens of the United States, or subjects of their Allies, to their entire liberty, if any there be in the Choctaw nation. They shall also restore all the negroes, and all other property taken during the late war, from the citizens, to such person, at such time and place, as the Commissioners of the United States of America shall appoint, if any there be in the Choctaw Nation.

Article 2d. The Commissioners plenipotentiary of all the Choctaw Nation, do hereby acknowledge the tribes and towns of the said nation, and the lands within the boundary allotted to the said Indians, to live and hunt on, as mentioned in the third Article, to be under the protection of the United States of America, and of no other Sovereign whosoever.

Article 3d. The boundary of the lands, hereby allotted to the Choctaw nation to live and hunt on, within the limits of the United States of America, is, and shall be the following, viz. Beginning at a point on the thirty-first degree of North Latitude, where the eastern boundary of the Natches district shall touch the same; thence east along the said 31st degree of North latitude, being the southern boundary of the United States of America, until it shall strike the eastern boundary of the lands on which the Indians of the said Nation did live and hunt on the twenty-ninth of November, one thousand seven hundred and eighty-two, while they were under the protection of the King of Great-Britain. Thence northerly along the said eastern boundary, until it shall meet the northern boundary of the said lands; thence westerly along the said northern boundary,

On Motion of Mr. [Charles] Pinckney, seconded by Mr. [Edward] Carrington,

Resolved, That the Secretary at war direct the commanding officer of the troops, to detach two companies to the rapids of the Ohio, to protect the inhabitants from the incursions and depredations of the Indians.

On the question to agree to this resolution, the yeas and nays being required by Mr. [William] Grayson,

State / Member	Vote	State vote
New Hampshire,		
Mr. Long,	ay	}*
Massachusetts,		
Mr. Gorham,	ay	no
King,	no	
Dane,	no	
Sedgwick,	no	
Rhode Island,		
Mr. Manning,	ay	}*
New York,		
Mr. Haring,	ay	ay
Smith,	ay	
New Jersey,		
Mr. Symmes,	ay	ay
Hornblower,	ay	
Pennsylvania,		
Mr. Pettit,	ay	ay
Wilson,	ay	
Maryland,		
Mr. Henry,	ay	ay
Hindman,	ay	
Harrison,	ay	
Virginia,		
Mr. Grayson,	ay	ay
Monroe,	ay	
Lee,	ay	
Carrington,	ay	
North Carolina,		
Mr. Bloodworth,	ay	ay
White,	ay	
South Carolina,		
Mr. Pinckney,	ay	ay
Huger,	ay	
Georgia,		
Mr. Few,	ay	}*

So it was resolved in the Affirmative.

[Motion of Mr. Grayson]

Motion,
June 22, 1786

Ordered that the Secretary for foreign affairs be directed to transmit to the Executives of ye States, abstracts of the numbers, names and owners of negroes carried away by ye British in contravention to ye late treaty of peace, and which were the property of ye Citizens of such States respectively.[1]

MONDAY, JUNE 26, 1786.

Congress assembled. Present, New Hampshire, Massachusetts, New York, New Jersey, Maryland, Virginia, North Carolina, South Carolina and Georgia; and from Pennsylvania, Mr. [John Bubenheim] Bayard.

Mr. Nathaniel Ramsay, a delegate for Maryland, attended, and took his seat in Congress.[2]

According to Order, Congress was resolved into a committee of the whole, to take into consideration the state of public affairs. The hon^ble^ Mr. [Samuel] Livermore was elected to the chair.

After some time, the president resumed the chair, and Mr. [Samuel] Livermore reported, that the committee have had under consideration the subject referred to them, but not having come to a conclusion, desire leave to sit again.

Ordered, That the committee sit again to Morrow.

[1] This motion, in the writing of William Grayson, is in the *Papers of the Continental Congress*, No. 36, III, folio 263. According to indorsement it made June 22 and "Referred to the Secretary for foreign Affairs to take Order." The motion and order thereon were also entered, by Thomson, in Committee Book No. 190 which notes "July 3 a letter from the Secy on this subject."

JUNE 22: The following committee was appointed: Mr. [William] Harrison, Mr. [John Cleves] Symmes and Mr. [William] Grayson, on a "Memorial of Jacob Rubsamen the settlement of his Acct." Report was rendered July 12.

Committee Book No. 190.

Also, on June 22, according to indorsement, was read the report of the committee of November 30, 1785, on the memorial of Lt. Col. Moses Rawlings. It is in No. 19, V, 231, in the writing of Charles Pinckney and was adopted practically verbatim June 30, where it is spread on the Journals.

[2] For credentials see *ante*, January 17, 1786.

JUNE 26: On this day Mr. [Samuel] Livermore was added to the committee of June 21, on the report of the Indian Commissioners, in place of Mr. [James] Wilson.

Committee Book No. 190.

Also, according to indorsement, was read a petition from Captain Duncan Campbell, praying the settlement of his accounts. It is dated June 14 and is in No. 42, II, folio 261. See *post*, June 28.

appear, that the best account is rendered of the articles purchased or received by the deceased, which present circumstances will admit of, that they be, and they hereby are authorised to direct the issue of the usual certificate for any balance which may appear due on the settlement of the cash account of the deceased.[1]

WEDNESDAY, JULY 5, 1786.

Congress assembled. Present, as before.[2]

Letter from John Jay, as read July 5, 1786

OFFICE FOR FOREIGN AFFAIRS,
3d July, 1786.

SIR: I find that Congress were pleased on the 22d Ult; to order me "to transmit to the Executives of the States Abstracts of the Numbers, Names, and Owners of Negroes carried away by the British in contravention to the late Treaty of Peace, and which were the Property of the Citizens of such States respectively."

[1] JULY 3: The following committees were appointed: Mr. [Josiah] Hornblower, Mr. [John Cleves] Symmes and Mr. [Melancton] Smith, on the "Report of board of treasy and Secy at War on claim of Capt. Baldwin." Report was rendered July 20. See *ante*, April 24.

A Grand Committee consisting of Mr. [Samuel] Livermore, Mr. [Nathan] Dane, Mr. [James] Manning, Mr. [William Samuel] Johnson, Mr. [Melancton] Smith, Mr. [John Cleves] Symmes, Mr. [Charles] Pettit, Mr. [John] Henry, Mr. [Arthur] Lee, Mr. [Timothy] Bloodworth, Mr. [Charles] Pinckney and Mr. [William] Houstoun, "To report such amendments to the Confederation and a draft of such resolutions as it may be necessary to recommend to the several states for the purpose of obtaining from them such powers as will render the federal government adequate to the ends for which it was instituted." Report was rendered August 7.

The "Report of Secy at War on claims of Jesse Cook and Jesse Grant" was referred to the Commissioner of Army Accounts to report and report rendered July 6.

"A motion of Mr. [William] Houstoun respectg lieut Col. Pannill of the Georgia line" was referred to the Commissioner of Army Accounts to report and report rendered August 1.

Committee Book No. 190.

[2] JULY 5: "Motion of Mr. [Charles] Pettit for extending the resolution of May 10, 1780, to certificates lost out of the bounds of U. S." was referred to the Board of Treasury to report and report rendered August 9.

Committee Book No. 190.

I suspect that Congress were not apprized of the Length of this Account. A very diligent and good Clerk in this Office was employed six Weeks in making a Copy of it for M[r] Adams. The Number of Clerks now in the Office are barely sufficient for the ordinary Business of it. If therefore thirteen manuscript Copies are to be made, with any tolerable Degree of Expedition, it will be necessary for me to employ a large additional Number. The Expence will be considerable, and the Means of defraying it being rendered uncertain by the present State of the Treasury, which is now in arrear, even to the stated Clerks, creates Difficulties which merit consideration.

This Account does not appear to me capable of Abridgement, and I am inclined to think that the Wages of extra Clerks would exceed the Price for which it might be printed.

That Congress may judge of these Circumstances with greater Precision I herewith transmit the Book in which this Account is entered.

Whatever may be the Orders on this or any other Subject, it will always give me Pleasure to execute them with Punctuality and Expedition.

I have the Honor to be etc.

JOHN JAY.[1]

His Excellency,
The President of Congress.

THURSDAY, JULY 6, 1786.

Congress assembled. Present as before.

On a report of the secretary at war and commissioner for army accounts, on the memorial of Jesse Cook and Jesse Grant,

OFFICE OF ARMY ACCOUNTS,
July 6th, 1786.

The Commissioner for Settling the Accounts of the Army to whom was referred the Memorial of Jesse Cook and Jesse Grant, begs Leave to report:

[1] This report is in the *Papers of the Continental Congress*, No. 80, III, folio 21. According to indorsement it was read July 5 and referred to Mr. [Charles] Pinckney, Mr. [William] Grayson and Mr. [Timothy] Bloodworth, who reported July 6. The report was acted on August 9.

That by Virtue of a resolution of your honorable House of the 16th of April, 1781, Your Commissioner hath settled the Accounts of the Memorialists, who have been allowed their Old emission money agreeable to the usual mode of paying the Army and also their Subsistence from which was deducted the Supplies made by the Commissary of prisoners.

That your Commissioner omitted the settlement of their depreciation in Consequence of the above mentioned resolution and also their pay after the first of August, 1780, to the date of their exchange, for the reason that the state of Connecticut settled with Line for that time,

That your Commissioner in his settlement with these Officers considered the Warrant of the Governor of the State and the Certificate of the Secretary at War that they were appointed Captains to be a Sufficient Authority for him to settle their Accounts as such so far as they lay in his department.

That the Memorialists have Obtained their Depreciation and pay from the State of Connecticut, as Lieutenants, but their petition for the difference between the depreciation of Lieutenants and Captains has for some reason unknown to your Commissioner been negatived by the Legislature of the State.

And Therefore that the real Subject of Complaints of Memorials, and which the report of the Secretary at War has a tendency very justly to remove is that the State be Authorized to Settle with them as Captains and Lieutenants.

JNO. PIERCE.[1]

Resolved, That it be recommended to the state of Connecticut, to settle with Jesse Cook and Jesse Grant, late

[1] This report is in the *Papers of the Continental Congress*, No. 62, folio 145. According to indorsement it was read July 6. The report of the Secretary at War was read June 1.

Also, according to indorsement, was read the report of the committee of July 5 on the lists of negroes carried away by the British. It was adopted August 9 and is there spread *verbatim* on the Journal.

Reading of a committee report, July 6, 1786

JULY 6: The following committee was appointed: Mr. [James] Monroe, Mr. [William Samuel] Johnson, Mr. [Charles] Pinckney, Mr. [Rufus] King and Mr. [Nathan] Dane, on "The report of the board of treasy viz. Requisition for 1786." This was the report dated June 22 and read June 27, for the consideration of which July 5 had been assigned. See *post*, August 2.

Committee Book No. 190.

Resolved, That the sum of thirty dollars be allowed to Jeremiah Jackson, William Alexander, Robert Wilkin, Blackall William Ball, Edward Butler, and James Gilchrist, late officers in the Pennsylvania line, respectively, to defray travelling charges from the Southern Army in March, 1782.

On the report of a committee, consisting of Mr. [Charles] Pinckney, Mr. [William] Grayson and Mr. [Timothy] Bloodworth, to whom was referred a letter from the Secretary for foreign Affairs.

Resolution, August 9, 1786

Resolved, That the Secretary for foreign Affairs cause to be made out separate lists of the numbers, names and owners of the Negroes belonging to the citizens of each State, and carried away by the british, in contravention of the late treaty of peace: and that he transmit the said lists to the executives of the States to which they respectively belong.

The Committee appointed under the resolution of 27 of July last submit the following report in part:

Resolv'd, * * *

That a Committee be appointed to confer with the said Legislature as soon as it shall be conven'd, to state to them the exhausted and embarrased state of the publick finances and in consequence thereof the eminent disadvantages which must result to the Union from her failure to comply with the said recommendation.[1]

[1] This report, in the writing of James Monroe, is in the *Papers of the Continental Congress*, No. 24, folio 423. According to indorsement it was read August 9 and passed August 11 where the omitted portions are spread *verbatim* on the Journal. Roger Alden's indorsement states "Comm[ee] app[d] to confer with Legislature of Pens[a] respecting the Impost Law." See *post* August 14.

August 9: The following committees were appointed:

Mr. [Rufus] King, Mr. [Melancton] Smith, Mr. [Pierse] Long, Mr. [William Samuel] Johnson and Mr. [John] Bull, on "Motion of Mr. [Rufus] King for abolishing Com[rs] for settling betw: U. S. and ind: states and appointing a board of three for that and other purposes." See *post*, September 5.

Mr. [Edward] Carrington, Mr. [Charles] Pinckney and Mr. [Nathan] Miller, on "Report of Com[r] of Army Acco[ts] on Mem[l] of Marinus Willet." A report was rendered August 17. See *ante*, May 24, Pierce's report is indorsed as referred to the Board of Treasury for a report and report rendered and passed March 21, 1787.

A motion was this day made by Mr. [Nathan] Miller regarding the committee report on the Algerines. See *ante*, August 8. *Committee Book No. 190.*

On motion of Mr. [Charles] Pinckney, seconded by Mr. [John] Henry,

Resolved, That the board of treasury be, and they are hereby directed, to advance to the secretary at War, one thousand dollars; he to be accountable.[1]

Submission of an act of Georgia, September 29, 1786

The delegates for Georgia, laid before Congress an Act of that state, in pursuance of the recommendation of the 30 April, 1784, passed the 2d of August, 1786, vesting the United States in Congress assembled, for the term of 15 years, commencing on the day Congress shall begin to exercise the powers, with a power to prohibit the importation or exportation of goods, wares or merchandize, in ships belonging to, or navigated by subjects of powers with whom the U. S. shall not have formed treaties of Commerce, and to prohibit the subjects of foreign states, unless authorised by treaty, from importing goods, wares or merchandize which shall not be the produce or manufacture of the dominion of the sovereign whose subjects they are, provided that nine states agree in the exercise of this power, and that it do not extend to prohibit the importation of negroes, and that the Act shall not have force until the other twelve states have substantially complied with the recommendation above mentioned.[2]

The Commissioner for settling the Accounts of the late Army, to whom was referred the Petition of George Thompson, Executor, to the Estate of the late Genl Wm Thompson, begs leave to report that the Petitioner's Demand for rations of the General from the 8th of June, 1776, the time of his being made a Prisoner, to the 3d of September, 1781, when he died, is attended with some difficulties; the principal of which is that the General Officers of the Army not being confined to one ration daily as was the case of the regimental officers, have drawn from different Commissaries, such quantities of Provisions on Account, as they found necessary for the supply of their respective Tables. That but few if any of those Gentlemen ever kept any regular account of their drafts upon the Commissaries, and that the Accounts of that department (as will appear by Mr. Burrell's Letter to your Commissioner accompanying this report) are in such a situation that they cannot furnish such Information as may

[1] This motion, in the writing of Charles Thomson, is indorsed on Knox's letter of September 29, above.

[2] An exemplification of this act of Georgia is in No. 76, folio 282.

same shall be laid before the said board, within one year after the organization thereof, the board shall examine the same, and report the state of such claims, with their Opinion thereon to Congress.

That the Commission of the board shall continue in force for three years, unless sooner revoked by Congress. Done, &c.

OFFICE FOR FOREIGN AFFAIRS,
October 13, 1786.

The Secretary of the United States for the Department of Foreign Affairs, to whom was referred a Letter of the 4th March last, from the Hon[ble] John Adams, Esquire, together with the papers that accompanied it, reports,

That as the subject of these papers and of this report appears to your Secretary in a very important point of light, he thinks they should be so incorporated as that the record of the latter in this Office may always exhibit an entire and complete view of the whole business. He therefore reports,

That on the 8th day of December, 1785, Mr. Adams, agreeable to his instructions of the 7th day of March, 1785, presented to His Britannic Majesty's Secretary of State a Memorial, dated the 30th day of the preceding month, in the following words:

Memorial presented by John Adams to Great Britain, as reported by the Secretary of Foreign Affairs, October 13, 1786

A MEMORIAL

The Subscriber, Minister plenipotentiary from the United States of America, has the honour to represent to the Ministry of His Britannic Majesty, that by the seventh Article of the preliminary treaty of peace between his Majesty and the United States of America, signed at Paris, on the thirtieth day of November, one thousand seven hundred and eighty two, confirmed by the definitive treaty of peace, signed at Paris, on the 3[d] day of September, one thousand seven hundred and eighty three, it was stipulated, that his Britannic Majesty should, with all convenient speed, and without causing any destruction, or carrying away any Negroes or other property of the American Inhabitants, withdraw all his Armies, garrisons and fleets from the said United States, and from every port, place and harbour within the same, leaving in all fortifications the American Artillery that may be therein.

That, although a period of three years has elapsed since the signature of the preliminary treaty, and of more than two years since that of the definitive treaty, the posts of Oswegatchy, Oswego, Niagara, Presque-isle, Sandusky, Detroit, Michillimackinac, with others not necessary to be particularly enumerated, and a considerable territory round each of them, all within the incontestable limits of the said United States, are still held by British garrisons, to the loss and injury of the said United States.

The subscriber, therefore, in the name and behalf of the said United States, and in obedience to their express commands, has the honor to require of his Britannic Majesty's Ministry, that all his Majesty's Armies and garrisons be forthwith withdrawn from the said United States, from all and every of the posts and fortresses herein before enumerated, and from every other port, place and harbour, within the territory of the said United States, according to the true intention of the treaties aforesaid.

Done at Westminster, this thirtieth day of November, one thousand seven hundred and eighty five.

JOHN ADAMS.

Resolutions of General Assembly of Virginia, as presented in a report of the Secretary of Foreign Affairs concerning Britain's failure to live up to the treaty of peace, October 13, 1786

VIRGINIA TO WIT.

In General Assembly, the 22d of June, 1784.

It appearing to the General Assembly from a Letter from His Excellency General Washington, dated the 7th day of May, 1783, that in obedience to a resolution of Congress, he had a conference with General Carleton, on the subject of delivering up the Slaves and other property belonging to the Citizens of the United States, in compliance with the Articles of the provisional treaty; that he (General Carleton) appeared to evade a compliance with the said Treaty, by a misconstruction of the same, and permitted a large number of the said Slaves to be sent off to Nova Scotia. It further appearing to the General Assembly, from the testimony of Thomas Walke, Esquire, that he together with several other persons from the Counties of Norfolk and Princess Anne, in or about the month of April, 1783, went to New York, with a view of recovering the Slaves which had been taken from them by the british troops during the war; that not being permitted to take possession of those Slaves, which they found in that City, the said Walke made a personal application to General Carleton, and requested a delivery of the said Slaves in compliance with the seventh Article of the treaty which prohibits the carrying off Negroes, or other property, belonging to inhabitants of the United States. This he peremptorily refused, alleging that he was not authorized to do it without particular instructions from the british Government; that at the time of this application the said Walke was informed by an Aid de Camp of General Carleton, that an Agent was appointed to superintend the embarkation, and keep a register of Slaves sent to Nova Scotia; and that he afterwards saw the said register, and also saw a large number of Negroes embarked to be sent to that Country. It further appearing to the General Assembly from the testimony of Mr. John Stewart, of the State of Maryland, as well as from a variety of other circumstances, that many applications were made to General Carleton, by Citizens of America, for the restitution of property, which were invariably rejected:

Resolved, That there has been an infraction on the part of Great Britain, of the seventh Article of the treaty of peace between the United States of America and Great Britain, in detaining the Slaves and other property of the Citizens of the United States.

Resolved, That the Delegates representing this State in Congress be instructed to lay before that body the subject matter of the preceding Information and resolution, and to request from them a remonstrance to the british Court, complaining of the aforesaid infraction of the treaty of peace, and desiring a proper reparation of the injuries consequent thereupon; that the said Delegates be instructed to inform Congress, that the General Assembly has no inclination to interfere with the power of making treaties with foreign nations, which the Confederation hath wisely vested in Congress; but it is conceived, that a just regard to the National honor and interest of the Citizens of this Commonwealth obliges the Assembly to withhold their co-operation in the compleat fulfilment of the said treaty, until the success of the aforesaid remonstrance is known, or Congress shall signify their sentiments touching the premises.

Resolved, That so soon as reparation is made for the aforesaid infraction, or Congress shall judge it indispensably necessary, such Acts of the Legislature passed during the late War, as inhibit the recovery of british debts, ought to be repealed, and payment thereof made in such time and manner as shall consist with the exhausted situation of this Commonwealth. Extract from the Journal of Assembly.

John Beckley,
Clerk H. Ds.

Inasmuch therefore as laws of Virginia, existing in force after the peace, *did inhibit the recovery of british debts,* there can be no doubt, but that such inhibition was and is an infraction of the 4th Article of the Treaty. Whether that infraction was justifiable, or in other words, whether the reasons assigned for it in the preamble to those resolutions were good and sufficient, shall be considered under a distinct head.

As to the Bill said to have passed the Legislature of Virginia, in October, 1784, the Complainants admit that it never became a law, and therefore it is, and ought to be, entirely out of question.

North Carolina is classed with Virginia in such a manner as to infuse an idea of her having given occasion to similar complaints, but not a single charge being specified or stated against her, there is reason to presume that she had not given just cause for Complaint. Whether that is or is not in fact the case, your Secretary is uninformed, not having as yet been able to procure a Copy of the Acts of North Carolina.

Of *South Carolina* the list of grievances complains in strong and pointed terms. It takes particular notice of an Ordinance passed there the 26th March, 1784, vizt

AN ORDINANCE RESPECTING SUITS FOR THE RECOVERY OF DEBTS.

Be it ordained by the honourable the Senate and House of Representatives met in General Assembly, and

of and in pursuance of the said recited act, in the common Goal of Charleston district:"

"*And Whereas* such persons have severally preferred their humble petitions to the Legislature of the said State, asserting their innocence of any of the Crimes imputed to them, and praying for a trial and full examination of their Conduct, which petitions have been received and are referred to proper Committees, by both houses of the Legislature: *And Whereas* it is considered unnecessary in such cases, to carry the said in part recited Act into a full and strict execution, with respect to the close imprisonment and sale of the effects of the said persons as aforesaid surrendering and submitting themselves. And the Legislature, with its accustomed lenity, hath resolved to admit bail for such persons to be taken to enforce their appearance at a future day, when the merits of their petitions shall have been decided on."

The Act accordingly admits them to Bail, and suspends the further sale of their estates until their cases should be finally decided on. To this Act there is annexed, "A List of persons on the Confiscation Bill who have petitioned, and whose cases have been favorably determined in the Senate, and others who have been favorably reported on in the House of Representatives." This List contains above seventy names; the Complainants however seem not to have been of that description.

In the same session another good natured Act was passed, which among other things provided, "that the household furniture, plate, linen, wearing apparel, Carriages and Carriage horses, with such Negroes as were generally attendant upon the family of those

Act of South Carolina of March 16, 1783, as presented in a report of the Secretary of Foreign Affairs concerning Britain's failure to live up to the treaty of peace, October 13, 1786

persons who were described in the Confiscation Act, *should be allowed to them.*"

Your Secretary takes notice of this Act because it indicates a degree of humanity in the Legislature which, considering the outrages committed in that State, is remarkable.

On the 17th March, 1783, an Ordinance was passed for disposing of the estates of certain persons, and for other purposes therein mentioned. It recites, "that many of the former Citizens of that State in violation of their allegiance had withdrawn themselves, and joined the enemy." It Confiscates the estates of such persons. It directs the Commanding Officers of the several Regiments of Militia to return the names of such persons to the Commissioners within three months. With great regard for justice and fairness, it permits such persons to return to the State within six months after the *end* of that session, *to take their trial*, and declares the Ordinance to be void as to such of them as should be acquitted.

If the Complainants were of the class mentioned in this Act, they either neglected the means it prescribes for them to manifest their innocence, or they failed in doing it.

On the 26th March, 1784, an Act was passed which in the opinion of your Secretary places the magnanimity and moderation of the State in so distinguished a point of light, that it ought to be inserted at large in this report.

"An Act for restoring to certain persons therein mentioned, their estates, both real and personal, and for permitting the said persons to return to this State, and for other purposes therein mentioned.

in the said Lists No. 1, 2 and 3 comprehended, shall be liable and subject to pay all Commissions and Charges which may be due to the Commissioners of forfeited estates, or others acting under their authority. And in any instance where the Negroes or other property of any person hereby subject or liable to amercement hath been sold or taken, or moneys have been received by virtue of any law or publick authority of this State, the price for which such Negroes were sold, and the value of such other property and money received as aforesaid, shall be allowed in discount of their amercement respectively.

Act of South Carolina of March 26, 1784, concerning disposition of forfeited estates, as presented in a report of the Secretary of Foreign Affairs concerning Britain's failure to live up to the treaty of peace, October 13, 1786

And be it further enacted by the authority aforesaid, That the several persons whose names are contained on the List No. 3, and all such on the List No. 1, who held military Commissions at any time during the war, be disqualified from being elected Governor, Lieutenant Governor, Member of the privy Council, or of either branch of the Legislature, or of holding any Office or place of trust within, or under the authority of this State, for and during the term of seven years.

And Whereas several persons have applied to the Legislature to be relieved from the penalties of an Act entitled "An Act for amercing certain persons therein "mentioned," whose petitions are referred to a Committee of each branch of the Legislature:

Be it therefore enacted by the authority aforesaid, That as much of the said Act as respects the several persons favourably reported on in either House, shall be, and the same is hereby repealed. And that the operation of the said Act shall be suspended as to the remainder of the said persons therein mentioned, until the end of the next meeting and sitting of the Legislature.

Report of the Secretary of Foreign Affairs concerning Britain's failure to live up to the treaty of peace, October 13, 1786

There is no doubt but that Britain has violated the 7th Article, which provides "that his Britannic Majesty shall with all convenient speed, and without causing any destruction, or carrying away any Negroes, or other property of the American Inhabitants, withdraw all his Armies, garrisons and fleets from the said United States, and from every post, place and harbour within the same."

The Violations of this Article alluded to, are these, viz[t]

1. That on the evacuation of New York, Negroes belonging to American Inhabitants were carried away.

2. That his britannic majesty's Garrisons have not been withdrawn from, but still keep possession of certain posts and places within the United States.

With respect to the Negroes, it may be proper to distinguish them into *three* Classes.

1. Such as in the course of the War were captured and disposed of as booty by the Enemy.

2. Such as remained with and belonged to American Inhabitants within the british lines.

3. Such as, confiding in proclamations and promises of freedom and protection, fled from their Masters without, and were received and protected within, the british Camps and lines.

The stipulation, "not to carry away any Negroes or other property of the American Inhabitants," cannot in the opinion of your Secretary be construed to extend to, and comprehend the *first* Class. By the laws of war all goods and Chattels captured and made booty *flagrante Bello*, become the property of the Captors. Whether men can be so degraded as under any circumstances to be with propriety denominated Goods and Chattels, and under that idea capable of becoming booty, is a question on which opinions are unfortunately various, even in Countries professing Christianity and respect for the rights of mankind. Certain it is that our Laws assert, and Britain by this Article as well as by her practice admits, that Man may have property in Man. If so, it is fair reasoning to conclude that this like other moveable property is capable of changing Owners by capture in War. The Article places "Negroes and other property of the American Inhabitants" on the same footing; so that if it means that Captured Negroes shall not be carried away, it must also mean that no other captured property shall be carried away, which would in other words amount to an agreement that the british fleet and Army should leave behind all the booty then in this Country, which they had taken from the American Inhabitants at any period of the War. It would be a task beyond the abilities of your Secretary to raise such a construction of the Article on any principles capable of supporting it.

As to the *Second* Class, to wit, such as belonged to and remained with American Inhabitants within the british lines, they seem clearly to be within the design and meaning of the Article; for as the enemy had never taken them from their Masters, nor treated them as booty, the property remained unchanged; and the like reasoning applies to all other Negroes kept as Slaves within their lines, and respecting whom the enemy had done no Act which divested their Masters of the property.

Your Secretary also thinks that the *third* Class are clearly comprehended in the Article, and for the same reason, Viz[t] because they still remained as much as ever the property of their Masters. They could not by merely flying or eloping extinguish the right or title of their Masters; nor was that title destroyed by their coming into the enemy's possession, for they *were received, not taken* by the enemy; they were received not as Slaves but as friends and freemen; by no Act, therefore, either of their own or of their friends, was the right of their Masters taken away; so that being the property of American Inhabitants, it was an infraction of the 7th Article of the treaty to carry them away.

Whenever the conduct of Nations or of Individuals becomes the subject of investigation, truth and candor should direct the enquiry. The circumstances under which these last mentioned Negroes were carried away make a strong impression on the mind of your Secretary, and place that transaction before him in a point of view less unfavourable to Britain than it appears in to his Countrymen in general. He is aware he is about to say unpopular things; but higher motives than personal considerations press him to proceed.

If a War should take place between France and Algiers; and in the course of it France should invite the American Slaves there to run away from their Masters, and actually receive and protect them in their Camp, what would Congress, and indeed the world, think and say of France, if, on making peace with Algiers, she should give up those American Slaves to their former Algerine Masters? Is there any other difference between the two cases than this, Vizt that the American Slaves at Algiers are *white* people, whereas the African Slaves at New York were *Black* people?

It may be said that these remarks are made out of season; for whether they be well or ill founded, the fact is, that Britain expressly agreed to give them up, and therefore ought to have done it.

How far an obligation to do wrong may, consistent with morality, be so modified in the execution as to avoid doing injury, and yet do essential justice, merits Consideration. By this agreement Britain bound herself to do great wrong to these Slaves; and yet by not executing it she would do great wrong to their Masters. This was a painful dilemma; for, as on the one hand, she had invited, tempted and assisted these Slaves to escape from their Masters, and on escaping had received and protected them, it would have been cruelly perfidious to have afterwards delivered them up to their former bondage, and to the severities to which such Slaves are usually subjected; so on the other hand, after contracting to leave these Slaves to their Masters, then to refuse to execute that Contract, and in the face of it to carry them away, would have been highly inconsistent with justice and good faith. But one way appears to your Secretary in which Britain could extricate herself from these embarrassments, that was, to keep faith with the Slaves by carrying them away, and to do substantial justice to their Masters by paying them the value of those Slaves. In this way neither could have just cause to complain; for although no price can compensate a Man for bondage for life, yet every Master may be compensated for a runaway Slave.

In the opinion therefore of your Secretary, Great Britain ought to stand excused for having carried away these Slaves, provided she pays the full value of them; and on this he thinks the United States may with great propriety and justice insist. Indeed there is an intimation in one of Mr. Adams's Letters, that the British Minister did not object to it.

But however capable of palliation the conduct of Britain respecting these Negroes may be, it unquestionably was an infraction of the 7th Article.

It is equally clear, that her continuing to hold the posts from which by that Article she agreed to withdraw her Garrisons, is also a decided violation of the Treaty.

It appears, then, that there are violations of the Treaty justly chargeable on both parties; but as the present inquiry is, whether our violations can be justified by antecedent ones on the part of Britain, their respective dates must be ascertained.

It is but just to observe, that Britain withdrew her fleet and Army from New York before the treaty was ratified. She evacuated that place on the 25th November, 1783; and it was not until the next year that the treaty was ratified.

The first violation that (to the knowledge of your Secretary) we complain of, happened when the British forces left New York; for they then carried away with them the Negroes in question; so that the first violation on the part of Britain was on the 25th November, 1783.

The famous trespass Act of New York was passed 17th March, 1783, and is still in force.

The Act of Pensylvania, which impeded the recovery of british debts, was passed 12th March, 1783.

The Ordinance of South Carolina for disposing of certain estates, &c. was passed 17th March, 1783.

All these acts were in force on and long after the day of the date of the treaty, Viz[t] 3d September, 1783.

In whatever light, therefore, deviations from the Treaty prior to its final conclusion and ratification may be viewed, it is certain that deviations on our part preceded any on the part of Britain; and therefore instead of being justified *by* them, afford excuse *to* them.

91716°—VOL 31—34——27

Recommendations of the Secretary of Foreign Affairs concerning the minister to Great Britain, in his report on Britain's failure to live up to the treaty of peace, October 13, 1786

That he also be authorized to propose and conclude, in the name and behalf of the United States, a Convention with his Majesty, whereby it shall be agreed, that the value of the Negroes, or other American property carried away contrary to the 7th article, be estimated by Commissioners, and paid for; and that the said payment, together with a surrender of all the posts and places now held by his Majesty within the limits of the United States, shall be within Months after all the Acts and parts of Acts existing in the several States, and which violate the treaty, are repealed, and due notice thereof given.

That he be also instructed to assure his Majesty that it will always give pleasure to Congress fairly and candidly to discuss and accommodate every difference or Complaint that may arise relative to the construction or to the performance of the treaty. That they are determined to execute it with good faith; and that as this is the only instance in which any Complaints of that kind have ever come regularly before them, they flatter themselves that the frankness and Candor of their conduct on this Occasion will create in him the same confidence in the purity of their intentions, which they repose in his assurance, "that whenever America shall manifest a real determination to fulfil her part of the treaty, Great Britain will not hesitate to co-operate in whatever points depend upon her for carrying every Article into real and complete effect."

It might also be well to instruct Mr. Adams to endeavour to have an Article inserted in the Convention for the remission of the interest, or a proportion of it, which became due on private Contracts during the War; but your Secretary apprehends, from the general and great impropriety of such interference with private Contracts, that his endeavours would be fruitless.

Letter from John Jay, as read April 13, 1787

[Report of Secretary for Foreign Affairs on instructions to Mr. Adams [1]]

OFFICE FOR FOREIGN AFFAIRS
23d April 1787

The Secretary of the United States for the Department of foreign Affairs in obedience to the order of Congress directing him to report Instructions to their Minister Plenipotentiary at the Court of London, on the Subject of his Letter of 4th March 1786, and of the Papers which accompanied it,

Reports the following

Resolved That the Minister of the United States at the Court of Great Britain, be, and he hereby is, instructed to inform his britannic Majesty, that Congress do candidly admit, that the 4th and 6th Articles of the Treaty of Peace have been violated in America, and that they consider the 7th Article as having been violated on the part of Great Britain. That he do also inform his britannic Majesty, that Congress are taking effectual measures for removing all Cause of Complaint on their part, and that he communicate to his Majesty their Resolutions of the 21st Day of March last, together with their circular Letter to the States of the 13th Day of April ~~Instant.~~

Resolved That the said Minister be, and he hereby is authorized and directed, in the name and Behalf of the United States to propose and conclude a Convention with his Majesty, whereby it shall be agreed that the value of the Slaves or other American Property carried away contrary to the 7th Article, be estimated by Commissioners and paid for, and that the said Payment, together with a Surrender of all the Posts and Places now held by his Majesty within the Limits of the United States shall be made within months after the several States shall each have passed such a Law for repealing all the Acts or parts of Acts existing in the same and repugnant to the said Treaty, as is specified in the circular Letter above mentioned, which months shall be computed from the Time that formal notice, of all the States having passed such Laws, shall be duly given to his britannic Majesty.

Resolved That the said Minister be, and he hereby is, further instructed to assure his Majesty that it will always give pleasure to Congress fairly and candidly to discuss and accommodate every Difference or Complaint that may arise relative to the Construction or

[1] *Papers of the Continental Congress*, No. 81, III, pp. 97–99, read April 23, 1787. See March 21, July 18, and 20, 1787.

be a less number of free Inhabitants in the State than sixty thousand.

Article the Sixth. There shall be neither Slavery nor involuntary Servitude in the said territory otherwise than in the punishment of crimes, whereof the party shall have been duly convicted; provided always that any person escaping into the same, from whom labor or service is lawfully claimed in any one of the original States, such fugitive may be lawfully reclaimed and conveyed to the person claiming his or her labor or service as aforesaid.

The Northwest Ordinance, as read for the third time and passed July 13, 1787. Underlining indicates words added to the original report by amendments during debate

Be it Ordained by the Authority aforesaid, that the Resolutions[1] of the 23d of April 1784 relative to the subject of this ordinance be, and the same are hereby repealed and declared null and void.

[2] Done &c.

On passing the above Ordinance the yeas and nays being required by Mr [Abraham] Yates

Massachusetts		
Mr Holten	ay	ay
Mr Dane	ay	
New York		
Mr Smith	ay	
Mr Haring	ay	ay
Mr Yates	no	
New Jersey		
Mr Clarke	ay	ay
Mr Schurman	ay	
Delaware		
Mr Kearny	ay	ay
Mr Mitchell	ay	
Virginia		
Mr Grayson	ay	
Mr R H Lee	ay	ay
Mr Carrington	ay	
North Carolina		
Mr Blount	ay	ay
Mr Hawkins	ay	
South Carolina		
Mr Kean	ay	ay
Mr Huger	ay	
Georgia		
Mr Few	ay	ay
Mr Pierce	ay	

So it was resolved in the affirmative.

[1] *Journals*, vol. XXVI, pp. 275–279.
[2] Charles Thomson resumes the entry.

[1] On the report[2] of a Committee to whom was referred a report[3] of the Secretary for foreign Affairs of the 23[d] of April last respecting instructions to the minister of the United States at the Court of London,

Resolved That the minister of the United States at the Court of Great Britain, be and he is hereby instructed to inform his Britannic Majesty that Congress have taken measures for removing all cause of complaint relative to the infraction of the 4th and 6th Article of the treaty of peace, and that he communicate to his Majesty their resolutions of the 21st March last together with their circular letter to the States, of the 13th day of April.

Resolution regarding claims to Britain for carrying away slaves, July 20, 1787

Resolved That the said Minister be and he hereby is authorised and directed in the name and behalf of the United States to propose and conclude a Convention with his Britannic Majesty whereby it shall be agreed that the value of slaves or other American property carried away contrary to the 7th Article of the Treaty of peace be estimated by Commissioners;[4] and that he also endeavor to obtain an Article to fix the true construction of the declaration for ceasing hostilities, and to

[1] From this point to the end of the day the proceedings are entered by John Fisher and attested by Charles Thomson in *Secret Journal Foreign, Papers of the Continental Congress*, No. 6, III, pp. 380–383. The vote in this entry is by states only. The proceedings are also entered by Thomson in *Secret Journal, Foreign Affairs, Papers of the Continental Congress*, No. 5, III, pp. 1613–1616.

[2] See July 18 and 19, 1787.

[3] See April 23, 1787.

[4] At this point the following was struck out from the original report: "and paid for and that the s[d] Payment together with a surrender of all the Posts and places now held by his Majesty within the limits of the U S shall be made within months after the several States shall have passed an act [or Acts] in conformity to the resolutions beforementioned, which months shall be computed from the time that formal notice shall be given his Majesty that all the States have passed an act [or Acts] as above mentioned." *Papers of the Continental Congress*, No. 25, II, p. 474. See the motions below.

stipulate that compensation be made for all Captures contrary to it.

Resolved That the said minister be and he hereby is further instructed to assure his Majesty that it will always give pleasure to Congress fairly to discuss and accommodate every difference or complaint that may arise relative to the construction or to the performance of the Treaty. That they are determined to execute it with good faith. And that as this is the only instance in which any complaints have come regularly before them they flatter themselves that the readiness with which they have taken measures to remove these complaints will create in him a full confidence in the purity of their intentions, and that he assure his Majesty that they fully repose and confide in his assurances "that whenever America shall manifest a real determination to fulfil her part of the treaty Great Britain will not hesitate to co-operate in whatever points depend upon her for carrying every Article into real and compleat effect."

CHA^s THOMSON *Sec^y*

In debating the foregoing Resolutions a motion was made by M^r [Melancton] Smith seconded by M^r [William] Grayson to amend the second resolution by adding thereto as follows (after the word Commissioners)

"And that the payment for the same together with a surrender of all the posts and places now held by his Majesty within the limits of the United States shall be made within a certain reasonable time after the several States shall have passed an Act or Acts in conformity to the resolutions before mentioned, and formal Notice shall be given his Majesty that all the States have passed an Act or Acts as above mentioned."

Blessings of Liberty to ourselves and our Posterity, do ordain and establish this Constitution for the United States of America.

ARTICLE. I.

SECTION. 1. All legislative Powers herein granted shall be vested in a Congress of the United States, which shall consist of a Senate and House of Representatives.

SECTION. 2. The House of Representatives shall be composed of Members chosen every second Year by the People of the several States, and the Electors in each State shall have the Qualifications requisite for Electors of the most numerous Branch of the State Legislature.

No Person shall be a Representative who shall not have attained to the Age of twenty five Years, and been seven Years a Citizen of the United States, and who shall not, when elected, be an Inhabitant of that State in which he shall be chosen.

From the U.S. Constitution, as submitted in the report of the Convention of the States, September 20, 1787

Representatives and direct Taxes shall be apportioned among the several States which may be included within this Union, according to their respective Numbers, which shall be determined by adding to the whole Number of free Persons, including those bound to Service for a Term of Years, and excluding Indians not taxed, three fifths of all other Persons. The actual Enumeration shall be made within three Years after the first Meeting of the Congress of the United States, and within every subsequent Term of ten Years, in such Manner as they shall by Law direct. The Number of Representatives shall not exceed one for every thirty Thousand, but each State shall have at Least one Representative; and until such enumeration shall be made, the State of New Hampshire shall be entitled to chuse three, Massachusetts eight, Rhode Island and Providence Plantations one, Connecticut five, New York six, New Jersey four, Pennsylvania eight, Delaware one, Maryland six, Virginia ten, North Carolina five, South Carolina five, and Georgia three.

When vacancies happen in the Representation from any State, the Executive Authority thereof shall issue Writs of Election to fill such Vacancies.

The House of Representatives shall chuse their Speaker and other Officers; and shall have the sole Power of Impeachment.

130052°—VOL 33—36——8

SECTION. 3. Treason against the United States, shall consist only in levying War against them, or in adhering to their Enemies, giving them Aid and Comfort. No Person shall be convicted of Treason unless on the Testimony of two Witnesses to the same overt Act, or on Confession in open Court.

The Congress shall have Power to declare the Punishment of Treason, but no Attainder of Treason shall work Corruption of Blood, or Forfeiture except during the Life of the Person attainted.

ARTICLE IV.

SECTION. 1. Full Faith and Credit shall be given in each State to the public Acts, Records, and judicial Proceedings of every other State. And the Congress may by general Laws prescribe the Manner in which such Acts, Records and Proceedings shall be proved, and the Effect thereof.

SECTION. 2. The Citizens of each State shall be entitled to all Privileges and Immunities of Citizens in the several States.

A Person charged in any State with Treason, Felony, or other Crime, who shall flee from Justice, and be found in another State, shall on Demand of the executive Authority of the State from which he fled, be delivered up, to be removed to the State having Jurisdiction of the Crime.

From the U.S. Constitution, as submitted in the report of the Convention of the States, September 20, 1787

No Person held to Service or Labour in one State, under the Laws thereof, escaping into another, shall, in Consequence of any Law or Regulation therein, be discharged from such Service or Labour, but shall be delivered up on Claim of the Party to whom such Service or Labour may be due.

SECTION. 3. New States may be admitted by the Congress into this Union; but no new State shall be formed or erected within the Jurisdiction of any other State; nor any State be formed by the Junction of two or more States, or Parts of States, without the Consent of the Legislatures of the States concerned as well as of the Congress.

The Congress shall have Power to dispose of and make all needful Rules and Regulations respecting the Territory or other Property belonging to the United States; and nothing in this Constitution shall be so construed as to Prejudice any Claims of the United States, or of any particular State.

SECTION. 4. The United States shall guarantee to every State in this Union a Republican Form of Government, and shall protect

Read	*Acted on*	*Reports.*
Oct. 16	Feby 20	E Hunter's claim for money stolen referred to board of treas^y^
	transferred O	B. Harwood, claim for signing money
	transferred	G. Hands claim for exp. in separate Command
	transferred	d° for cloathing
	transferred	Halsted for supplies furnished in Canada
	transferred. O.	Journals of Congress, for reprinting
Oct. 26	transferred O	Lawrence and Morris respect^g^ the board of treas^y^
Oct 18	transferred	Capt M^c^Lean's claim
	transferred. O	Massachusetts disqualifying motion
	transferred	G Measam's *will*
	transferred	Militia plan recommended
	transferred O	Post Office for raising a revenue from
June 15	transferred	Ordinance for establishing
Aug 28	transferred O	Lady Sterling's claim for balance due
Oct 5	transferred O	Capt' Stewart and Cady's claim
18	Octr 25, 1787	Ja^s^ Smith's claim
Aug 4	transferred O	Revd R. Smith
Oct. 10	Feby 20	Genl S^t^Clairs claim referred to com^r^ for Army Acco^ts^ to take order.
June 15	transferred	Secretary at War his powers
	13 July 1787	Slavery to prevent it
	transferred	Chas Stockley
Oct 30	transferred O	Virginia Gov^rs^ letter respect^g^ Indians
	transferred O	John Weiss, drum major recommended to Rhode Isl^d^
	transferred O	Mary Wooster, her half pay
	transferred	Hez^h^ Whitmore, farther allowance to be made him
Aug 26	Feby 20th	Marinus Willet, pay and subsistance of his regiment referred to board of treas^y^.
Sept 19	transferred. O	Western Country temporary governm^t^ Motion of Mr Monroe grand Com^ee^ report on
	transferred O	Western posts
	transferred O	Genl Washington, allowance to
		List of Reports obsolete or negative
	transferred	John Buhler, for old cont. Currency
	transferred	Count Beaufort for obtaining a tract of land.
	transferred	Canadian and Nova Scotia Refugees
	transferred	Val: Eckharts claim
	transferred	Nath. Fuller's d°
	transferred O	Florat de florimont d°
	transferred	A Hutchins

List of reports, Appendix

[Motion of delegates of Georgia on cession of lands[1]]

The Delegates of the State of Georgia having laid before Congress, an act[2] of the legislature of that state empowering the delegates thereof to cede to the United States the claim of the said state to a certain tract of western territory. And the said Delegates having represented to Congress that they are ready to execute a deed of cession in compliance with said act,

Resolved, That Congress are ready to accept the cession of the claim of the State of Georgia to the tract of country described in the act of the said State, whenever the Delegates will execute a deed conformable to the said act.[3]

FRIDAY, MAY 30, 1788.

Congress assembled present New hampshire Massachusetts, New York, New Jersey, Pensylvania, Delaware Virginia, South Carolina and Georgia and from Rhode island M^r^

[1] *Papers of the Continental Congress,* No. 30, p. 597, in the writing of Mr. Abraham Baldwin. According to the *Committee Book, Papers of the Continental Congress,* No. 190, p. 192, the motion and the Act of Georgia were referred to a committee consisting of Mr. Abraham Clark, Mr. Nathan Dane, Mr. Hugh Williamson, Mr. Alexander Hamilton and Mr. Edward Carrington. Mr. Hamilton was replaced by Mr. Paine Wingate on June 24. The committee report was delivered July 9 and read July 14, 1788. See July 15, 1788.

[2] *Papers of the Continental Congress,* No. 76, pp. 292–295, certified copy read May 29, 1788. A certificate of the Governor is on p. 290 and a map of the lands ceded on p. 298.

[3] May 29, 1788. According to indorsement and the *Committee Book, Papers of the Continental Congress,* No. 190, p. 192, was referred to the Secretary for Foreign Affairs to report:

Georgia resolution concerning fugitive slaves, referred to Secretary of Foreign Affairs, May 29, 1788

A resolution of the House of Georgia, in session of January 30, 1788, respecting fugitive negroes, who fled to Spanish territory. *Papers of the Continental Congress,* No. 76, pp. 268–269 (certified copy), with a certificate of the Governor on p. 266 and a letter of Governor Zespedes to the Governor of Georgia, December 12, 1784, pp. 272–273 with translation on pp. 276–277. Report rendered August 15 and acted on August 26, 1788. Under this last date these papers were entered in a footnote in the *Secret Journal, Foreign Affairs, Papers of the Continental Congress,* No. 5, III, pp. 1699–1700.

According to indorsement was read:

Memorial of John Macpherson, respecting building of an impregnable fort, finding out of longitude and constructing a church. *Papers of the Continental Congress,* No. 41, VI, pp. 504–506. The receipt for the return of the plan of the fort, dated June 28, 1791, is on p. 508.

The Sec^y of Congress reports

Ag^d That the letter of the 8 from the Sec^y for foreign affairs with the papers therein enclosed be referred back to the Sec^y for foreign affairs to report.

On the letter[1] of 2 June last from Mess N and J Van Staphorst, which was transmitted to Congress the 12 inst by the Sec^y for foreign affairs and in which Messrs Van Staphorst earnestly desire to be furnished with a compleat sett of the Journals of Congress as a mean of providing in the best manner the monies necessary to support the credit of the United States until the new government can be organized and operate to this effect; And to lay the foundation for transferring to the money lenders in Holland the debt due by the US to the crown of France.

Ag^d The Sec^y of Congress reports That the letter of the 2 June from Messrs Van Staphorst be referred to a Com^ee.[2]

On the petition[3] of W Imlay Comm^r of the loan Office for the state of Connecticut representing the incompetency of his salary and the inequality of it compared with that of others and the business done in his office and praying for relief,

The Sec^y of Congress reports

Ag^d That the petition of W Imlay Com^r of the loan office for the State of Connecticut be referred to the board of treasury to report.

Report of Secretary of Foreign Affairs, as read August 15, 1788

[Report of Secretary for Foreign Affairs on Georgia resolutions[4]]

OFFICE FOR FOREIGN AFFAIRS
14th August 1788

The Secretary of the United States for the Department of foreign Affairs, to whom was referred a Resolution of the House of Assembly

[1] See August 13, 1788.

[2] According to the *Committee Book, Papers of the Continental Congress*, No. 190, p. 202, this committee consisted of Mr. Hugh Williamson, Mr. Abraham Clark and Mr. Nathan Dane.

[3] According to the *Despatch Book, Papers of the Continental Congress*, No. 185, IV, p. 38, the petition was received (read) August 14, 1788.

[4] *Papers of the Continental Congress*, No. 81, III, pp. 79–80, read August 15, 1788. See May 29, August 20 and 26, 1788.

of Georgia of the 30th January last, with a Letter from Governor Zespedes, dated at St Augustin in Florida 12th Decemr 1784,

Reports.

That from these Papers it appears that sundry negroe Slaves belonging to Citizens of Georgia had fled to East Forida, and were there protected and detained.

That Application had been made on the Subject to the Governor of East Florida, and that although he has permitted those Fugitives to be apprehended and put in the keeping of Persons named by their Masters, yet that he cannot deliver them up without Instructions from his Court, which he has solicted, it having heretofore been the Practice of Florida not to deliver such Fugitives to Georgia, because the latter while under the british Government had refused to observe a reciprocal Conduct in that Respect.

That although in his Opinion these and similar Matters cannot be conveniently regulated but by Treaty, yet that for the present it would be proper to send Copies of these Papers to the Chargé des Affaires of the United States at Madrid, and instruct him to represent to his Catholic Majesty the Inconveniences which the States bordering on his Dominions experience from the Asylum afforded to their fugitive Slaves, to solicit his Orders to his Governors to permit and facilitate their being apprehended and delivered to thier Owners or to Persons authorized to receive them, and to assure his Majesty that the said States will observe the like conduct respecting all such Slaves belonging to his Subjects as may be found therein.

That it also appears to him expedient to communicate these Papers to the Encargado de Negocios of Spain and that it be signified to him by your Secretary, that his Interposition to obtain proper Regulations to be made on this Head, would be very agreeable to Congress.

All which is submitted to the Wisdom of Congress.

John Jay.[1]

[1] August 15, 1788. According to the *Committee Book, Papers of the Continental Congress*, No. 190, p. 202, the following committee was appointed:

Mr. Hugh Williamson, Mr. Samuel Allyne Otis and Mr. Abraham Baldwin on their report of August 12, 1788, on the application of George Morgan. Report rendered August 28, 1788. See June 25, July 1, 8, 15. 30 and August 11, 1788.

According to indorsement was read:

Letter of Thomas Hutchins to President of Congress, August 15, 1788, announcing his departure for the Western territory. *Papers of the Continental Congress*, No. 60, p. 339.

urge Congress to authorise the Commissioner appointed to receive the Accounts of the said State against the U.S, to admit as authentic documents, the Books of the Treasurer and Auditor in support of claims for advances of money ~~for the~~ on account of the said U. S. from the 1^{t} of Sep^{t} 1775 to the 4th of Jany 1781, the Vouchers for the said advances during that Period having been distroyed or burnt by the Enemy in Arnolds Invasion.

Therefore *Resolved* that the Commissioner appointed to receive the accounts and vouchers of the state of Virginia against the U. S., be and hereby is directed and authorised to admit the Books of the Auditor and Treasurer of the said State as authentic documents to validate the claims thereof for monies advanced on account of the U. S. from the 1st of September 1775 to the 4th of Jany 1781 in all cases where it shall appear to the satisfaction of the said Commissioner that the vouchers have been destroyed as set forth by the said General Assembly.[1]

[1] AUGUST 20, 1788. According to the *Committee Book, Papers of the Continental Congress*, No. 190, p. 203, the following committees were appointed:

Mr. Abraham Clark, Mr. Hugh Williamson, Mr. Abraham Baldwin, Mr. Jeremiah Wadsworth and Mr. Alexander Hamilton on their report on the contract with Jarvis for copper coins. See August 4, 1788. The committee reported September 16, 1788. See also July 16 and August 27, 1788.

Appointment of a committee concerning fugitive slaves, August 20, 1788

Mr. Alexander Hamilton, Mr. Theodore Sedgwick and Mr. James Madison on the report of the Secretary for Foreign Affairs on the resolution of Georgia respecting fugitive negroes. See August 15, 1788. The committee reported August 26, 1788.

Mr. Nathan Dane, Mr. Hugh Williamson, Mr. Abraham Clark, Mr. James Madison and Mr. Joshua Seney on the letter of the Governor of Virginia of August 4, 1788, respecting the Act of July 17, 1788. See August 14, 1788. The committee reported August 28, 1788. See also September 1, 1788.

Mr. Jeremiah Wadsworth, Mr. Alexander Hamilton and Mr. Abraham Clark on the report of the Board of Treasury on the claim of Joseph Spencer. See August 5 and 14, 1788. The committee reported September 30, 1788.

Also according to the *Committee Book*, was referred to the Board of Treasury to take order:

The committee report on the letter of the Board of Treasury, respecting the reservation of Presque Isle. See July 22 and 30, 1788. This report and the order thereon were entered by John Fisher in *Western Territory, Papers of the Continental Congress*, No. 176, pp. 60–61.

Resolution concerning recovery of fugitive slaves protected by Spain, August 26, 1788

[1] On the report [2] of the com^{ee} consisting of M^{r} [Alexander] Hamilton M^{r} [Theodore] Sedgwick and M^{r} [James] Madison to whom was referred a report [3] of the Secretary for the department of foreign Affairs of the 14th Instant,

Resolved, That the Secretary for the department of foreign Affairs be directed to transmit copies of the papers * referred to in his said report to the Chargé des

* GEORGIA

HOUSE OF ASSEMBLY
Wednesday the 30 Janu^{y} 1788.

On a Motion made by Mr William Few the House came to the following Resolution:

Whereas authentic information has been laid before this House that sundry negro Slaves belonging to Citizens of this State have absconded from their Masters and gone to East Florida where they are protected and detained from their rightful Owners by the Government of his most Catholic Majesty to the great injury of the Citizens of this State, contrary to the Usage of Nations in Amity, and those principles of friendship which this State wishes to preserve with the Subjects of his most Catholic Majesty.

Resolved, That the Letter of the Governor De Zespedes, dated the 12 of December 1784, be transmitted to the Delegates of this State in Congress, and that the said Delegates or either of them be and they are hereby instructed and required to lay a statement of the case before the United States in Congress Assembled, and to move that such measures may be taken on the occasion as will redress the injured Citizens of this State and remove the cause of such complaints.

[1] From this point to the end of the day the Journal entry was made by Charles Thomson and Roger Alden, with the notes by Benjamin Bankson in *Secret Journal, Foreign Affairs, Papers of the Continental Congress,* No. 5, III, pp. 1698–1700. The Journal entry proper was also made by John Fisher and attested by Charles Thomson in *Secret Journal Foreign, Papers of the Continental Congress,* No. 6, III, pp. 426–427.

[2] *Papers of the Continental Congress,* No. 25, II, pp. 499–500, in the writing of Mr. Alexander Hamilton. Read August 26, 1788. See August 20, 1788.

[3] See August 15, 1788. See also May 29, 1788.

Affaires of the United States at Madrid and instruct him to represent to his Catholic Majesty the inconveniencies

Extract from the minutes

JAS. M. SIMMONS, *Clk. G. A.*

MY DEAR SIR: The expressions your Excellency has honored me with in your Letter of 27 of October fills me with satisfaction, and I will certainly have the greatest pleasure at all times and on every occasion to manifest the true esteem I entertain of your Excellency and your Citizens.

With respect to the depredation of the English Subjects in cutting of Timber on the Island of Cumberland, I am to say, that, as the late Treaty of peace grants Eighteen months to the British to evacuate this province unmolested, I cannot during that space of time, disturb the existence of their transports in the River Saint Marys, nor at any time, take notice of the excesses that the Subjects of another Sovereign may commit in a territory that does not belong to me.

I have procured to Mr Coddington all the means in my power for the recovery of his Negroes which might eventually have come into this province; leaving it at his free election when recovered to deposit them, into the hands of a person of his choosing until I receive from the Court their Resolution which I have some time past applied for, concerning these identical Slaves; being obliged to conform myself, until I receive new Instructions, to the antient Regulations of this Government, one of which prescribes, not to disturb any fugitive Negro from Georgia, as the Court of London in that respect refused a reciprocal correspondence. At the same time, I have represented to his Majesty, that Georgia is differently circumstanced as not being as formerly a British Colony. And I expect anxiously an answer to my Representation, with a sincere desire to be authorized to comply fully with the Requisitions of your Excellency.

I remain with the greatest Respect to your Excellency, praying God preserve your life many years. Saint Augusta in Florida 12 December 1784.

I kiss your Excellency's hand, being your most acknowledged, hum Serv.

VIZ MANL DE ZESPEDES.

His Excellency
THE GOVERNOR OF GEORGIA

which the States bordering on his dominions experience from the Asylum afforded to fugitive negroes belonging to the citizens of the said States; And that Congress have full confidence that orders will be given to his Governors to permit, and facilitate their being apprehended and delivered to persons authorised to receive them; assuring his Majesty that the said States will observe the like conduct, respecting all such negroes belonging to his Subjects as may be found therein.

Resolved, that the said Secretary be also directed to communicate the said papers to the Encargado de Negocios of Spain, and to signify to him, that his interposition to obtain proper regulations to be made on the subject, would be very agreeable to Congress.[1]

[2] WEDNESDAY, AUGUST 27, 1788.

Congress assembled present Massachusetts New York New Jersey, Pensylvania, Delaware, Maryland, Virginia South Carolina and Georgia and from New hampshire M^r [Paine] Wingate from Connecticut M^r [Benjamin] Huntington and from North Carolina M^r [Hugh] Williamson.

[Report of committee on the memorial of J. Lawrence [3]]

The Committee consisting of [Mr. Hugh Williamson, Mr. Paine Wingate, Mr. Nathan Dane, Mr. William Few and Mr. Nathaniel Mitchell] to whom was referred the Memorial of Jesse Lawrence beg leave to report.

[1] AUGUST 26, 1788. According to the *Despatch Book, Papers of the Continental Congress*, No. 185, IV, p. 38, were received and according to the *Committee Book, Papers of the Continental Congress*, No. 190, p. 204 were referred to the Board of Treasury to report:

Memorial of Udny Hay requesting the reimbursement of £79–2–3.

Petition of George Taylor, bellows maker, for the settlement of his account of retained rations.

[2] Charles Thomson resumes the entry.

[3] *Papers of the Continental Congress*, No. 19, III, pp. 489–490, in the writing of Mr. Hugh Williamson. Read and passed August 27, 1788. See August 25, 1788.

penditure, which no Funds at the command of the United States would be adequate to supply. They therefore Submit to the consideration of Congress the following Resolve.

That the application of Duncan Campbell for payment in Specie, of the Certificate ordered to be issued to him by the Commissioner of Army Accounts, by the Resolve of Congress of the 19th of Septemr 1786, cannot be complied with.

All which is humbly Submitted.

September 15th 1788.

SAMUEL OSGOOD
ARTHUR LEE [1]

WEDNESDAY, SEPTEMBER 17, 1788.

Congress assembled present as before.[2]

THURSDAY, SEPTEMBER 18, 1788.

~~Congress assembled~~ Six states only attending namely Massachusetts Connecticut New York Virginia North-Carolina and Georgia and from New hampshire Mr [Nicholas] Gilman from Rhode island Mr [Peleg] Arnold from Pensylvania Mr [James R.] Reid from Delaware Mr [Dyre] Kearny and from South Carolina Mr [John] Parker, the President adjourned Congress to ten oClock to morrow.

[1] SEPTEMBER 16, 1788. According to indorsement and the *Committee Book, Papers of the Continental Congress*, No. 190, p. 207, the following were read and referred:

Petition of Ezekiel Williams, August 14, 1788, for the repayment of money spent on care of prisoners. *Papers of the Continental Congress*, No. 42, VIII, pp. 447–452. Referred to the Board of Treasury to report. Report rendered October 1, 1788.

Petition of Joseph King, in behalf of Absolam Baird, September 16, 1788, requesting half pay and commutation, *Papers of the Continental Congress*, No. 42, I, p. 439. Referred to the Commissioner of army accounts to report. Report rendered September 25, 1788.

Appointment of a committee, September 17, 1788

[2] SEPTEMBER 17, 1788. According to indorsement and the *Committee Book, Papers of the Continental Congress*, No. 190, p. 207, the following committee was appointed:

Mr. Abraham Clark, Mr. Hugh Williamson and Mr. James Madison, on the memorial of B. Tardiveau, agent of the inhabitants of St. Vincents and Illinois, September 17, 1788, requesting modifications in resolutions of Congress. Report rendered September [25] 1788. Cf. February 25, 1788.

[Report of committee on land bounties for officers[1]]

The Committee consisting of Mr [Abraham] Clark Mr [Edward] Carrington and Mr [Nathan] Dane to whom were referred a report of the Secretary at War, report,

That Congress by their Acts [2] of the 16th and 18th of Septemr 1776, granted bounties of Land to the Officers and Soldiers who had engaged or should engage in the Service, and continue therein to the end of the War, or untill discharged by Congress and to the representatives of such Officers and Soldiers as should be slain by the Enemy. That upon a New Establishment of the Army in 1778, many of the officers at that time in Service were left out as Supernumerary, in Consideration whereof it was on the 24th of Novemr in said year, *Resolved*, That Congress gratefully Acknowledge the faithful services of such Officers, and that all Supernumerary Officers be entitled to one years pay of their commissions respectively, to be computed from the time such Officers had leave of Absence from the Commander in Chief on this account. That whatever might have been the intention of Congress, your Committee cannot find it any where declared or intimated that the allowance of one years pay should be considered as a full compensation for their services, or intended in any wise to exclude them from their bounties of Land; whereupon the following resolution is Submitted,

That the Secretary at War be, and he is hereby instructed to consider all those officers who became Supernumerary by the Arrangement of the Army in the years 1778 and 1779, As entitled to the bounties of Land granted by Congress in Septemr 1776, and to issue Warrants accordingly.

Committee report, September 25, 1788

[Report of committee on memorial of B. Tardiveau [3]]

The Comee consisting of Mr [Abraham] Clark Mr [Hugh] Williamson and Mr [James] Madison to whom were referred the memorial of Mr Tardiveau Agent of the French and American Inhabitants of the

[1] *Papers of the Continental Congress*, No. 27, p. 363, in the writing of Mr. Abraham Clark. Indorsed as read September 23, which is apparently an error. See March 12, July 17 and August 28, 1788.

[2] *Journals*, vol. V, pp. 763 and 781, respectively.

[3] *Papers of the Continental Congress*, No. 19, VI, pp. 9–10 in the writing of Mr. Abraham Clark. Read September 1788. As there is no indication of the day of the reading, this report is printed on the first day on which business was transacted after the appointment of the committee. See September 17, 1788.

Illinois and Post S[t] Vincents, report, that in and by the Ordinance [1] for the Government of the Western territory passed the 13th day of July 1787, it is ordained that, "there shall be neither Slavery nor involuntary Servitude in the said territory otherwise than in the punishment of Crimes whereof the party shall have been duly convicted. And Whereas since the passing of said Ordinance it appears there were at that time Negroes under Servitude to the inhabitants then residing at Kaskaskies Illinois Post S[t] Vincents and other of the Antient French Settlements whose Right to the property they possessed were guaranteed by Congress in their Act [2] Accepting the Cession [3] of Claim to Western territory made by the State of Virginia; which Right of property it was not the intention of Congress to violate by said Ordinance but merely to restrain the Settlers in future from carrying persons under Servitude into the Western territory, for remedy whereof,

Resolved, That the before mentioned Ordinance for the government of the Western territory, shall not be construed to deprive the Inhabitants of Kaskaskies Illinois Post S[t] Vincents and the other Villages formerly settled by the French and Canadians, of their Right and property in Negro or other Slaves which they were possessed of at the time of passing the said Ordinance, or in any manner to Manumit or Set free any such negroes or other persons under Servitude within any part of s[d] Western territory; any thing in the said Ordinance to the contrary notwithstanding.

And Whereas Congress by their Acts of the 20th of June and 29th of August last, took measures for confirming in their possessions and Titles all the French and Canadian Inhabitants and others, Settlers at or near the Rivers Mississippi Illinois and Wabash, who on or before the year 1783, had professed themselves Citizens of the United States or any of them, and for laying off the several tracts which they rightfully claim within certain limits. And also in and by said Acts directed the laying of certain tracts of Land of such extent as to contain four hundred acres as ~~bounties~~ donations to each of the heads of families in the districts therein mentioned to be divided among them by lot, but omitted making any grants of land for Supporting

[1] *Journals*, vol. XXXIII, p. 343.

[2] *Journals*, vol. XXVI, p. 116.

[3] Original cession, engrossed on parchment, is in *Papers of the Continental Congress, Cessions of Western Lands.*

[Letter of Secretary for Foreign Affairs with letter of Mr. Gardoqui[1]]

OFFICE FOR FOREIGN AFFAIRS

22d Septr 1788

Sir: I have the honor of transmitting to your Excellency herewith enclosed, a Letter (and a translation of it) from Mr Gardoqui dated the 19th instant, and am with great Respect and Esteem, etc.,

JOHN JAY.

His Excellency THE PRESIDENT OF CONGRESS.

[Letter of Secretary for Foreign Affairs, on letters of the Governor of Virginia[2]]

OFFICE FOR FOREIGN AFFAIRS

19th Septemr 1788

SIR: The Absence of the Minister of France (with whom it appeared to me expedient previously to converse on the Subject of the Letters of 30th June and 2d July from his Excellency the Governor of Virginia) induced me to postpone reporting on them. He arrived Yesterday, and I have seen him this Morning. He is preparing to go immediately to Boston, and prefers leaving this Affair in its present State until his Return. The Delay will not in my Opinion be inconvenient, and therefore I took the Liberty of consenting to it.

With great Respect, etc.,

JOHN JAY

His Excellency
THE PRESIDENT OF CONGRESS.

Receipt of letters, September 25, 1788

[1] *Papers of the Continental Congress*, No. 80, III, p. 589. It is indorsed as read September 23, but entered in the *Despatch Book*, p. 40, as received (read) September 25, 1788. The letter of Diego de Gardoqui to Jay, is in *Papers of the Continental Congress*, No. 97, pp. 222–226, original Spanish with English translation on pp. 230–232. The letter refers to orders for apprehending J. Sullivan and communications made respecting fugitive negroes. According to the *Committee Book*, *Papers of the Continental Congress*, No. 190, p. 207, Gardoqui's letter was referred to the Secretary for Foreign Affairs to report. Jay's letter bears the indorsement, "Novr 23d 1789, recd from the office f. f. Affairs. the papers enclosed filed in the office of f. Affrs not reported on".

[2] *Papers of the Continental Congress*, No. 80, III, p. 585, read September 25, 1788. The letters of the governor of Virginia relate to the Ferrier question. See August 8, 1788.